THE SECRET OF SOVEREIGNTY

Women Choosing Leadership at Work and in Life

DEDE HENLEY

RAGNELLE PRESS

Ragnelle Press

17837 First Ave S., Suite 302

Seattle, WA 98148

THE SECRET OF SOVEREIGNTY

First edition

10 09 08 07 06 05   1 2 3 4 5

Printed in the United States of America

ISBN (cloth): 0-9763544-0-3

ISBN (pbk): 0-9763544-1-1

Library of Congress Cataloging-in-Publication Data

Henley, Dede

The secret of sovereignty : women choosing leadership at work and in life

Includes bibliographical references and index.

ISBN 0-9763544-0-3 (cloth.)   0-9763544-1-1 (pbk.)

1. Business 2. Leadership 3. Women's Issues

I. Title. II. Title: The secret of sovereignty

Library of Congress Control Number 2005900316

Cover design by Peter Richards, interior design by Shannon McCafferty

www.dedehenley.com

Contents

Acknowledgments · v

Introduction · 1

1. Sovereignty: Your Claim to Freedom · 11

2. The Seven Deadly Traps for Women Leaders ·27

3. The First Secret: Follow Your Passion · 65

4. The Second Secret: Be Your Own Number One Priority · 77

5. The Third Secret: Reclaim Your Power · 95

6. The Fourth Secret: Create a Life of Adventure! · 131

7. The Fifth Secret: Keep Good Company · 145

A Parting Blessing · 157

Recommended Resources for Sovereign Women Leaders · 159

Bibliography · 161

Index · 162

Acknowledgments

This book has been a work in progress for many years and has been touched and influenced by so many people in my life. I am most grateful to my devoted editor, Ceci Miller, who with her combination of grace, encouragement, and perseverance made my ruminations into a book I am proud of.

I have had the privilege to work with thousands of women over the years, and to each of you I offer my deep gratitude. Thank you for sharing your struggles and triumphs, your dreams and disappointments. I bless the women who participated in the women's groups that helped shape this book. You have been my teachers and this book is written for you.

There are three women I hang out with to regain my own power and freedom. We call ourselves the "YooHoo Sisters"— loosely after *The Divine Secrets of the YaYa Sisterhood.* My sisters Jean Oplinger, Marnie Gustavson, and Carol Zizzo offer me friendship, courage, and clarity that sustain me.

My mother, the source of my life, has supported me in big and small ways. She has taught me the true meaning of generosity and selflessness. I acknowledge my father for being a seeker all his life and for passing on his love of learning to me. That he watches from heaven's gate is of great comfort to me.

I honor my teachers and guides whose words and work are reflected in this book. First, my beloved teacher and coach, Sheila Peralta. She has coached me and my family for more than eight years. That I found her was Divine intervention. Her extraordinary example, her willingness, and her pure delight in life have shaped the leader, woman, and mother that I am. I am eternally grateful for her partnership in this lifetime. My brother on the path, Garth Alley opened my heart to the medicinal feminine and a world of love and light. He is a true healer.

I received my training in leadership and organization development from two remarkable institutions. The first is the Pepperdine MSOD program. My teachers were Walt Ross, Miriam Lacey, Dick Beckhard, Peter Block, Bill Dyer, Billy Alban, Peter Koestenbaum, Barbara Bunker, and many others. The program attracts the best of the best in our field, and I had the good fortune to get to sit at their feet and learn from them. My development at Landmark Education Corporation provided the finest leadership training I have ever participated in. The distinctions and insights fundamentally altered the way I see and engage in life. Indeed, the work gave me a life I love.

As a consultant, my clients often become my family. None has been more dear to me than my family at DaVita. They changed my understanding of what is possible in organizations. Doug Vlchek "Yoda," Joe Mello, Kent Thiry, Ginny Coscarelli, Kathie Winter, and Foster Mobley deserve my deepest gratitude. I am grateful for their partnership and willingness.

A powerful woman is always surrounded by powerful women. I am blessed to have gathered a rich and true circle of friends: Patty Shortreed, Suzanne Lahl, Rosa Carillo, Linda O'Brien, Judy Todd, Erin Dorsey, Susanne Matheson, Mim Henley, Theresa Henley, Kathy Milne, and Perrianne Karstetter. These women fill my life with love.

To our children: Bryce, Carly, Blake, Jerremy, Christopher, and Spencer. They have graciously supported my ideas and fully participated in our family's growth. They are generous, loving and wise. They are the family I lean into for my strength and courage. I do all of this work for them.

Last and most important, I acknowledge my life partner, Steven Norris. He has remained faithful to love. His dedication to freedom has given me mine. He is my hero.

Introduction

Sovereignty is the freedom to choose—something, it seems, that we all want more of. Over the past several decades, increasing numbers of women have been gaining their freedom: at home, at work, in their families. Despite the once-popular belief that "it's a man's world," women are now shouldering greater challenges than ever before, reaching unprecedented levels of influence and personal mastery. The qualities that the world so desperately needs right now, the leadership skills strong enough to lead us into a new era—adept collaboration, willingness to do whatever it takes, and the ability to navigate diverse roles and relationships—are the very areas in which women most naturally excel. To move forward as a collective, the world needs women in leadership.

A new brand of women leaders is on the rise. They are those groundbreakers who have learned how to blend their natural leadership competencies with the archetypal energies of the feminine. Historically in our patriarchal culture, being a leader and being a woman have seldom been synonymous. Our challenge now as women is to step up and step in. The world needs what we have to offer, and it is our obligation to give it. Of course, we have much to learn and many choices to make. How can we make the transition from peer to leader, with all the relational ramifications that implies? How can we make the right choice, even when others may react by feeling left behind or betrayed? How, as leaders, can we honor ourselves and continue to remain faithful to our highest values? Such questions can never be answered with mere intelligence but only through wisdom. They are the timeless questions all leaders have faced.

To own and wield the wisdom of leadership is to claim ourselves, to recognize the strong force that we already are, to stop falling into the traps of social conditioning that would keep us small, and to stand in full sovereignty over our own lives.

Women's choices to date have mostly been to "fit in" or to "fall out." Many of us sold out by becoming "one of the boys." Being one of the boys worked, but it often meant giving up our real selves for someone more likely to be perceived as successful, smart, strategic, and savvy according to the boss and his priorities. We ended up feeling competent but lonely. Now women are beginning to yearn deeply for that which is real. We want to know what creates true strength. And this is where we begin the adventure of *sovereignty*: the secret of true leadership.

As I write, I'm on a train headed from Munich to Paris. The French countryside is an exquisite backdrop for the discourse I most love: women, leadership, choice, and true power. Never having traveled internationally on my own before, at first I was terribly afraid to take this trip. But intuitively I felt I would learn a great deal by this adventure independent of my life partner and children. So often when I am with them I tend to their needs and not to my own, falling into bed at night so exhausted I couldn't name my own needs if my life depended on it. This is part of the social conditioning we must learn to bring into balance, the early training that so often confuses women. We're taught to sacrifice our own needs in order to attend to the needs of our loved ones (see chapter 2, "The Seven Deadly Traps for

Women Leaders"). This overseas trip I'm taking now, a gift to myself, is exactly what I need to break the spell of insignificance; proof positive of my ability to meet my own needs powerfully on the stage of the world.

In the years I have spent studying women and leadership, I have found myself continually stunned at the low level of self-care, the extreme self-doubt, and the lack of true confidence that plagues so many women leaders. Even those who keep a brash public front are often brutally self-critical in the privacy of their own thoughts. But whether women are leading a team, defining a strategy, managing a project, or running a company, very few if any of us seem to have found a definitive map. How can we live as leaders in the world of work while continuing to live out our full personhood as women? I believe that we must join together, as groups of women are now doing all over the world, to engage in conversation about what it takes to create an extraordinary life—to become the kinds of leaders we ourselves would be honored to follow.

Gaining leadership and choice as women begins with raising our self-awareness. You may have spent years studying and mastering the knowledge of your field, whether it is science, medicine, law, banking, or technology, yet you may have spent little or no time studying yourself. What do you love? What inspires you? What brings you despair? What do you believe in and how did you come to hold this belief? What is real and meaningful for you? What remains true when all else seems lost?

I recently asked a group of women leaders to consider why anyone would bother with self-knowledge, self-awareness. After all, you don't get a toaster for doing the difficult work of consciousness-raising! They struggled with the question a bit, but such struggle is good; it's a sure sign of growth. I invite you to wrestle with this question for yourself. Why do the work? Why challenge yourself, your beliefs, your customary ways of doing things? Why move out of your comfort zone? Unless you can answer these questions well for yourself, you're not likely to venture very deeply into life's waters. To experience that depth—in your career, in your relationships, and in every other area of life—*self*-knowledge must matter to you. You must believe that knowing yourself will make a difference. Great leaders know themselves because others rely on them, follow them. What they're made of, what drives their character, matters.

Though admittedly the road is tough at times, increasing your self-knowledge and choice gives you direct access to joy. Life becomes simpler, more truthful. You know your gifts, your weaknesses, your successes and failures. Because you know yourself, you become more loving and compassionate; you've labored to give these gifts first and foremost to yourself, and in this way you have more to offer the world, even if it is only your peaceful presence. You become a blessing to all who have the great good fortune to cross your path. You are a true leader without apology. Though every woman's journey back to herself is different, unique, and uncharted, I invite you to say, *yes!* to your own journey. Answer the call willingly, with gratitude. This book will support you in that effort by offering helpful tools and giving you a place in which to reflect.

Balance and the Feminine at Work

During the past thirty years women have struggled constantly in our attempts to create balanced lives. The subject dominates the conversation among the executives with whom I consult. Balance seems to be the elusive modern-day Holy Grail. We want to rebalance our organizations, our families, and our marriages and partnerships. As we meet this challenge what is needed, in our organizations and our world, is a big dose of the feminine. We know that the masculine—its energies, its paradigms—has been the dominant operating paradigm on the planet for the past two thousand years or more. Our lives are not out of balance only individually, but collectively.

The feminist movement contributed to women's equality and helped women to receive acknowledgment in the workplace, placing well-deserved attention on an issue that had lain dormant for centuries. But although feminism began swinging the pendulum by challenging assumptions about the rights and roles of women, once again it may be time to get the pendulum swinging again. Women still comprise only 14 percent of the senior-level positions in organizations. The figure reveals an increase, it's true, but not one that statistically represents the total population of women in the workplace. Women in the workplace want more than the satisfaction of quotas. In our organizations we must bring to bear the myriad of resources, talents, and strengths that both genders possess. We must develop a balance.

The Masculine and Feminine Energies

Along with the assertion that what is missing from the modern equation is the expression of the feminine, I'll describe the masculine and feminine energies as I understand them. I am not speaking of male and female here. Both genders possess masculine and feminine qualities. When a man is compassionate, he is emanating feminine energy. When a woman is directing her energies in an efficient and focused way, she emanates the masculine. Most of us express an assortment of both masculine and feminine energies throughout the day. Our culture more often values and rewards masculine ways of being, however, and collectively we've become more masterful at this set of energies. Whether one inhabits a male or a female body, it is time to learn more about the powers of the feminine.

What is the feminine? It is inclusive, adaptive, yielding to the moment. It is not rigid or time-bound. The feminine flows easily from one energy, activity, or flavor into the next. The forces of nature are feminine. Think of places like Hawaii. Taking a walk on the beaches of lush Kauai, your whole body breathes fully, effortlessly filled with joy. The island is graced with double rainbows, the exotic calls of birds, and the fragrances of tropical fruit and flowers. The healing and rejuvenating ocean surrounds you. Here, feminine qualities abound: radiant, nurturing, beautiful, and healing. The feminine can also be wild and chaotic, like a hurricane or a thunderstorm. As we approach and understand the feminine we come to trust it, little by little, until at last we are able to call forth its energies consciously, with intention.

The masculine encompasses focus and accomplishment;

it's intensely directive and goal-oriented. The masculine may seem narrowly focused, yet it propels us into action and gets things done. In contrast to the fluid feminine, allowing all to flow freely around, within, and through it, the masculine tends to zero in on one thing at a time. Given a challenge, it can block out distractions and remain pointedly attuned with great clarity for hours at a time. The masculine may appear inflexible, more due to its power of focus than as a result of rigidity. The masculine thrives when it is trusted to be in charge. It likes to call the shots, to be relied upon. It *loves* a competition, a test of skill and prowess.

Does all this sound familiar? Male or female, it is the way we tend to approach the world of work. As a result of this imbalance of energies, many women have acquired an overdeveloped masculine aspect. Some women are no longer able to access their feminine selves. Women who adopted the ways of men in order to get along at work are afraid that if they show up as fully feminine, they may be considered flaky, or they may fear receiving a kind of attention they don't want. Historically, it has often been dangerous to fully honor the power of the feminine. (During the Catholic inquisition, the Church burned at the stake an astounding five million women over a period of three hundred years.) Little wonder that we abandoned our natural ways for safer, more culturally acceptable styles of operating in the world.

Now, however, we must take a second look at the results. Due to this excess of masculine expression in the workplace, women are leaving organizations in droves; they are burned out and sick. The canary in the cage is no longer singing! We simply can't keep living through the veneer of the masculine anymore.

Organizations need the feminine—and the women who might be able to offer it are bailing out. When we retain the capacity to access our feminine leadership, we give ourselves, our work, and our world a precious gift. That gift begins when we claim our sovereignty.

The intention of this book is to hand you a scepter and seat you on the throne of your own life—not to usurp the masculine, but to balance it by returning to your native expression of feminine power. So many women feel at a loss as to how to reconnect with this aspect of themselves. I am intimately familiar with their struggle, having spent fifteen years recovering my own strength and my true self, my own hard-won feminine energy and compassion. The path has been immensely rewarding and, though it often presented seemingly insurmountable difficulties, I wouldn't have missed a single step.

I invite you now to journey with me to a land where you are empowered to claim your sovereignty, to lead your own life, and to lead others with wisdom. There you will find that your personal life is not different from the life you lead at work. Life is life, and it's yours to bring into balance. In the chapters that follow, you may recognize yourself in the stories I share of true-life women leaders coping with the very real challenges of our time. As you identify the losses you may have sustained on your journey, you can now also begin to reclaim what is yours. You *can* change your direction and your way of taking part in the worlds of work, home, and play. You can reclaim your feminine way of being. Like most of us, you may have become weary, but don't surrender to despair as you pursue this fundamental and transformative goal. Strengthen yourself for a battle. Access your fierceness. Whether you seek to transform your team, your business, your community, your family life, or the world at large, you must remain solidly grounded in purpose. If you are willing to work to develop yourself as a woman and as a leader, you are guaranteed the restoration of your birthright of sovereignty. Let the journey begin!

1

Sovereignty:
Your Claim to Freedom

One day King Arthur went out hunting with his men and his favorite nephew, Sir Gawain. Sir Gawain was a true and perfect knight, loyal and courageous, clean in thought, word, and deed. He rescued damsels in distress, took care of old ladies, righted wrongs, and brought justice and comfort wherever he could. He was also tremendously handsome, with a great sunburst of golden hair. One fine day they were riding through the forest, the men dressed only in their greens, without armor. While chasing a stag Arthur came to a place where he was unable to pass, for looming ahead was a giant knight by the name of Sir Gromer Somer Joure.

"Ah, Arthur," the huge fellow sneered, "and Gawain, too. I've had it in for you since you took my land from me. Well, now you're going to have to fight me. Enough of this Camelot baloney. I'm going to slice you to smithereens. Come on, fight! There's only one of me and two of you."

"Now, just wait a minute," said King Arthur. "You're a

knight, isn't that so?"

"Of course I'm a knight. Can't you tell?"

"Well, no true knight would ever attack unarmed men."

"Shucks," said the giant. "All right then, I'll offer you a challenge. You have one year from today to find the answer to a question."

"I love a challenge!" said King Arthur. "Bring on the question!"

"The question is . . ." the huge knight grinned with anticipation. "The question is, *What do women really want?*"

"Oh, no!" Arthur and Gawain exclaimed in unison.

"And a year from today, if you still haven't found the correct answer, you'll have to fight me and I'll surely kill you then. I'll mash you into dog food. And it will be quits forever for this Round Table drivel."

As the giant knight continued to rave, King Arthur and Sir Gawain escaped into the forest. Right away Sir Gawain had a good idea: the two of them should travel in opposite directions, venturing far into strange lands to put the question to every woman they met. Each would record all the answers he gathered, until the two could meet and compare notes before their time was up. And so for nearly a year, the brave knights polled the female populace far and wide.

"Excuse me, madam, but what do women really want?" Sir Gawain inquired of a likely matron in a market town.

"Well, what *I* really want is a nice fur coat and an even nicer, furrier man to go with it!"

"Little girl, what do women really want?" King Arthur asked a lovely child playing with a badly torn rag doll.

"*I* want someone to beat up my brother."

"Hello, there, old dame! What do women really want?" called Sir Gawain to a woman as she hobbled along the road, leaning on a gnarled cane for support.

"Oh, my young man, what *I* would adore is for someone to bring an onion roll and a little hot soup to me in the morning, to do the dishes and milk the cow . . ."

Approaching Camelot's red light district, Sir Gawain spotted the comely Margarita. When he asked her the question, she rolled her eyes and said, "Oh my, Sir, do you think I could ever really tell you?"

Sir Gawain made his way back to court, where he asked the question of Queen Guinevere, who replied with a broad grin, "Ask Lancelot. *He* knows!"

The two men met again in the eleventh month, the day before they were sworn to return with their answer to Sir Gromer Somer Joure. As they compared their findings, they grew more and more worried. Both knights sensed that they had not yet uncovered the true answer. Seized with an inspiration born of desperation, Gawain offered, "I've heard that in the forest of Inglewood there's a woman who sits by a well. She is wondrous wise, but wondrous strange. In the day that remains, I will seek her out and ask *her* the question."

Gawain journeyed through the dark forest until he found, huddled near a well, a shape that seemed to him to be vaguely female. He gently tapped her protruding hump.

"Excuse me Madam, but could you tell me, what do women really want?"

The shape whirled around, and there stood before him the ugliest woman he had ever beheld. She had little rat eyes, warts standing upon warts, a face as red as an innkeeper's, steely wires for hair, and eyebrows so long that she had braided them into the hair on her head. She boasted a fine mustache about the mouth, and in that mouth one tusk of a tooth pointed upward while another pointed down. She drooled, and her scent was altogether unique.

"My, aren't you a pretty fellow!" she cackled as she ogled this handsome man. "Well, I know the answer to your question, but what'll you do for me if I tell you?"

Gawain gulped. "On my honor as a true and perfect knight, I will do anything that you ask."

Hearing this vow, Dame Ragnelle (for that was her name) hooted with pleasure. "Will you marry me, then?"

Gawain paled. Valiant knight that he was, however, he agreed.

"Mind you, I mean to be wed wearing a beautiful dress in front of the whole court. I want a high mass and a bountiful feast to celebrate our union—not some hole-in-the-wall affair."

Gawain agreed.

"Don't look so glum, my love. Though I be foul, I be merry. Now, since you've agreed, I'll tell you the answer. What women really want is *sovereignty*. They want not to be subject to a man or to any other, but to wield the power of choice."

"Yes Madam, that sounds right. I'll arrange for our marriage, then." And with that Sir Gawain mounted his horse and headed back with the hard-won answer.

The next day King Arthur and his nephew met with Sir Gromer Somer Joure. They handed him their two books filled with answers, which the knight perused with growing contempt.

"You can't be serious! These answers are as ridiculous as you are. Now you'll have to fight me. Come, let's get to it."

Just as the giant was about to slice off his head, King Arthur countered, "But sir, we have one last answer to offer: What women really want is *sovereignty*."

"*Aaaghh!* You've been talking to my sister! The wretch, may she burn in hell! Well, have a nice day then. You're free to go." And with that, Sir Gromer Somer Joure mounted his horse and galloped, glowering, into the forest.

The wedding proceeded on schedule, with the hideous Dame Ragnelle dressed magnificently in white and the handsome Sir Gawain a vision in green and gold. Dame Ragnelle blew kisses to everyone as she went down the aisle, but so offensive was her breath that several people fainted as she passed.

At the altar the priest asked, "Do you, Sir Gawain, take this . . . woman . . . to be your lawful wedded wife, et cetera?"

To which the gracious Sir Gawain answered, "On my honor as a true and perfect knight, I do."

The priest then asked, "Do you, Dame Ragnelle, take this poor, *poor* Sir Gawain to be your lawfully wedded husband, et cetera?"

"You'd better believe it, Toots. Now let's eat!"

The wedding banquet was a typical medieval feast: a stag stuffed with a boar, which was stuffed with a deer, which was stuffed with a woodchuck, which was stuffed with a partridge, which was stuffed with a hummingbird. Dame Ragnelle was beside herself with gluttonous glee. Drooling, she gnawed, gnashed, gobbled, and fairly inhaled her food, tearing at it with her grimy fingernails and long tusks. Those who dared to watch her eat lost their appetites on the spot. But no matter, for Dame Ragnelle finished everyone else's portion as well.

"Now it's time for bed!" she merrily announced as she finished her meal. Everyone at the table groaned.

But later, as the two newlyweds lay side by side beneath the sheets, the ghastly bride grew strangely shy. Sir Gawain lay there with his eyes tightly shut and his hands crossed over his chest like a man entombed in a stone sepulcher. Dame Ragnelle finally said, "Well?"

"Yes, Madam?"

"Aren't you going to do something?"

"Like what, Madam?"

"Well . . . you could give me a little kiss, maybe."

Sir Gawain blanched, but proved a true knight. "Yes Madam, I will do that . . . and I will do more."

"More? Oh, I like the sound of that *more*."

His eyes still closed, Sir Gawain leaned over and gave Dame Ragnelle a little peck on the cheek. Then, girding up his courage, he reached out a hand to touch her hair and then her face. But where there had once been steely, greasy wires, her hair now felt soft and lovely to the touch. And her skin—where were the warts? Where had this velvety skin come from? And where was the hairy boar's snout that had been her nose? Sir Gawain drew back and opened his eyes. There, lying next to him, was the most beautiful woman he had ever beheld. He stammered, "Wh-where is she? Where's Dame Ragnelle?"

The beauty replied, "Oh, my sweet husband. *I* am Dame Ragnelle."

The knight blinked. "You sure don't *look* like Dame Ragnelle!"

"That's because I was cursed by my wicked stepmother, who turned me into a hideous hag until the best knight in England would marry me and kiss me. But my dear, I'm afraid that isn't the end of the curse, for now you must make a choice. I can be beautiful for you at night and ugly to all others during the day. Or I can be beautiful to all others in the daytime and ugly for you at night. Which would you have?"

Sir Gawain weighed the alternatives. At last he said, "Madam, please, *you choose.*"

Dame Ragnelle threw her arms around Gawain's neck. "Ah, courteous knight, you have broken the entire spell by giving me sovereignty. Now I will be beautiful all the time." And then, as the story goes, they made merry together until midday.

What Is Sovereignty?

Fables and myths can point the way to important truths, to archetypal patterns in our lives that are otherwise difficult to see. The medieval story of Gawain and Ragnelle asserts that what all women truly want is *sovereignty*—the freedom to choose. With our sovereignty restored, women become "beautiful all the time." We discover, own, and express the best in ourselves. Living out this kind of self-sovereignty, this wholeness of being, would probably make for happier men, as well as women. We all want to make the choices truest to our nature. To do this, it is useful to explore the concept of sovereignty and its implications for us as women leaders.

Women and men have spent decades blaming each other for the pain caused by the very systems we have all helped to create. Feminists have railed against the status quo, in part to awaken men to the injustice of patriarchal systems, but above all to awaken women to their innate power of choice. Claiming and wielding the power of choice means *staying awake to our needs and wishes*—and therein lies the real work.

There are many ways to effect change. A company can begin from the outside and move in, by changing reporting and accountability structures, developing clear strategies, and intentionally shaping a culture that supports its employees. The trouble, though, is that many of us women have been waiting for positive changes to arrive from outside. We are waiting for the system itself to change. If we continue to wait, we may wait for a very long time. Experts say that on average, organization-wide change takes between seven and ten years. "Outside-in" reform *is* the most common path for planned change. But is it the most effective? Let's consider another way.

"Inside out" change begins with individuals changing their personal behaviors and values. For a leader to change the way she thinks, believes, and acts in the world means focusing on the effect she can have from within, regardless of external circumstances. In my experience, it is better for her to determine what she can change right now and then go after it, regardless of what seems to be happening around her. I'm not encouraging political recklessness here, rather a commitment to personal integrity and freedom. This change then naturally translates to a shift in interpersonal relationships and the ways in which people work together. Such changes roll up to adjustments within a team or group, until at length they help to drive new strategies that impact the entire organizational culture.

At work, as in our communities and families, women

must focus on inside-out change, then look to see how these changes cumulatively affect the overall structure. With inside-out change, you do not have to depend on anyone or anything else to change. You simply begin now. It has been said, "If you want to manage something, manage yourself." Wise counsel.

Consider first what may be holding you back from inside. Our heaviest albatrosses are often our limiting, unconscious conditioning—restrictive thoughts, fears, and concerns. Sovereignty, full choice, means freedom from such limits. Exercise free will in your life; give yourself full access. You may begin by identifying all the areas where you feel you don't yet have full freedom. Doing this, you begin to reclaim your power of choice.

Freedom occupies many domains. You may have financial freedom, religious freedom, physical freedom, sexual freedom. You may have enormous freedom to speak your mind, to express your emotions, to create a compelling future, or to strategize how to reach your goals, but you may have limited freedom in other domains. Where one woman has freedom, another may not; so we join together to show each other the way. Collectively, our range of choices expands. Observing the lives of others for inspiration, we envision what is possible as well as what is still left to be done.

It is the function of heroes to show us how great our lives can be *if we so choose.* Heroes hold up a standard, something we can strive for. That they have done it tells us that we can do it, too. Joseph Campbell's writings about the mythical hero archetype gave us a new language for understanding our life stories. He reminds us:

We have not even to risk the adventure alone. For the heroes of all time have gone before us. The labyrinth is thoroughly known. We have only to follow the thread of the hero path. And where we had thought to find an abomination, we shall find a God. And where we had thought to slay another, we shall slay ourselves. And where we had thought to travel outward, we shall come to the center of our existence. And where we had thought to be alone, we shall be with all the world.

When we insist on seeing ourselves as powerful, focused, and effective rather than waiting for the system to change, we step up as leaders. Remember that leaders go first; they don't wait. Waiting is for *followers*. Many women, however, are still moving about in the world—in our corporations, families, and communities—as though we were powerless martyrs and victims. Playing this lesser role leaves our characters undeveloped and our maturity stunted, no matter what our physical age may be. In many ways, waiting for change from outside of ourselves may seem a safe position. We watch and wait for power to be bestowed upon us. A true leader, however, is fully accountable, unafraid to exercise her *innate* power and wisdom. She is bold in offering her unique brand of leadership to the organization. She does not blame, make excuses, hide, or complain about circumstances beyond her control. She knows there is one source: herself. She claims her freedom by choice.

What Women Leaders Can Do Now
to Claim Sovereignty *Before* the System Changes

1. Follow Your Passion

Many of us do not fully express ourselves as women leaders. If we do gain access to our own authentic responses to life— and the enthusiasm that naturally goes with them—we are cautioned not to go overboard, to submerge our wildness, to avoid making waves.

I was working with an executive several months ago who had the most delightful laugh. I commented on it and told her how glad I was to be in her company. Hearing the compliment prompted her to share something that both touched and infuriated me. In her twenties, she had worked at a prestigious accounting firm. She had loved her job and the people there; she laughed often and enjoyed her work. She had always wanted to work in accounting and felt like she had found her dream job. Her boss, in a typical male-dominant accounting attitude, called her into his office. The look on his face told her she was being audited. He said, "Lose the laugh. It's not professional." She was crushed, but accepted this feedback as law. Ending her story she said, "I didn't laugh at work for fifteen years."

This powerful and joyful woman had abandoned something that was important and unique to her in the name of fitting in. So often and for so long women have done this, and in so many ways. For women, it is crucial to *belong*. We are relational creatures; we need the clan. We are willing to contort ourselves in many ways to avoid being ostracized. We may assume it's better to take our voices down a notch or two, just to insure ongoing membership.

If there are parts of your job that you don't love and don't feel naturally skilled at, find others who have the qualities you lack. The poet David Whyte said, "The Universe is holding its breath waiting for you to take your place in the pattern of things." We each have a unique place and a special set of skills to offer. Our first order of business must be to find and acknowledge them. Your gifts to the world as a woman leader are your birthright. When you live these gifts every day, in every interaction, your truest nature is expressed as an example to others. You become a hero and your fearlessness emboldens others.

2. Be Your Own Number One Priority

Women are notorious for putting the needs of others ahead of our own. We care for our children, our employees, our spouses, our friends, and our parents. Our own needs often fall to the bottom of this list, if they are attended to at all; then we wonder why we're exhausted and worn out. In our weariness, we entertain fairy tale fantasies that someday a white knight will whisk us away to someplace where life is easy.

Being *sovereign* means confronting the task of taking care of ourselves. This doesn't mean we're all alone without support or that no one cares about us. It simply means that we say and do whatever will make our lives workable. Being a powerful woman leader requires reserves of patience, energy, clarity, and passion. It means setting and maintaining clear boundaries. The deep well from whence these reserves can be constantly replenished is *self care*.

When you are your own number one priority, you know what you want and need in any given situation, and you go for it. You quickly and easily determine what does and doesn't work for you, and you let others know. You have the power to design a team, an organization, a life that works.

3. Knock Down Internal Walls

The walls we routinely put up to defend ourselves are far more confining than any physical walls. One of the biggest obstacles to your true leadership and sovereignty at work may be your own conversations. If so, you'll need to start getting out of your own way. Test the limits of the organization and your boss. Test your own limits. Play to win, instead of playing to not fail, lose, or look foolish. You may look foolish; you may fail. But you may well find it is self-imposed limitations, assumptions, and judgments that stop you from exercising your freedom. We play small because we don't want to rock the boat. Compromising ourselves to fit in, we thereby diminish our contribution, our clarity, and our creativity.

"Oh, I was just in the right place at the right time," we may offer apologetically. Women routinely undervalue our contributions and qualifications. We often don't ask for top dollar when negotiating salaries, benefits, or our daily rate. We're still uncertain whether we're worth it. That very uncertainty is writ large at work, where women in organizations continue to earn thirty cents less per dollar than men do. So where does the change begin? With changing the system? Perhaps. But I believe we must also change by beginning to value what women do.

I'm always surprised to hear the many internal limits that apparently powerful and successful women place on themselves. You wouldn't know it by looking at them. One Chief Operating Officer of a large bank doesn't feel she has the freedom to challenge her boss or the Board of Directors; she doesn't want to be seen as difficult or politically naïve. She stays quiet and controlled, leaving many of her ideas and thoughts unspoken. Another leader senses she needs mentoring to go to the next level but is afraid that seeking out a mentor might be perceived as a sign of weakness or an inability to fulfill her role. Being a leader with sovereignty means knowing that, fundamentally, you have the right to *be*. It means knowing that you matter, that you make a difference. Your becoming a leader involves getting out of your own way so you're free to offer your time, your talents, and your treasures. Ask for what you need. You don't have to shrink yourself to fit in.

4. Be Accountable

In order to become true leaders, we must take full accountability for every area of our lives. We must stop blaming ourselves or others for the results we experience at work or at home. Being accountable means knowing that you are responsible in some measure for everything that is in your life. Accountability means knowing you are answerable for your actions as well as your inactions. If questions come up or something goes wrong, consider your part in it. There's a subtle distinction between "It's not done" and "I haven't finished it." The willingness to be accountable for what you do and what you fail or refuse to do is essential to claiming sovereignty and inhabiting true leadership.

Victims and martyrs prefer to complain and suffer in silence. They blame others, the system, themselves. They hide behind doors, computers, paperwork, busyness, and other people. They say things like *I didn't know. I wasn't there. I don't have time. It's not my job. That's just the way I am. Nobody told me. It isn't really hurting anyone. I'm just following orders.* Victims and martyrs are quick to complain and slow to act. In organizations, such lack of accountability can derail a project or a team.

Consider what you haven't been willing to be accountable for in your own life. Think about the part you may have played in whatever isn't working. Claim this as yours and find one positive action to take. I call this an act of power. Doing this will return enormous choice and freedom to you. Victims believe there's nothing they can do in the face of external circumstances. When you have complete sovereignty you claim the full range of choices available to you. Choose well.

We must make many changes before our organizations can become places where women thrive. Some changes will come from adjusting the way in which we do business; other changes will come from within women themselves. Our challenge is to remain clear and resolute in our purpose. Change, for the most part, happens slowly. We must be patient then, and persevere. In *Freedom and Accountability at Work,* Peter Koestenbaum says, "A person who is free is a person who never gives up. They are always looking for the betterment of their life situation." We must promise not to give up on the idea that by claiming our sovereignty—our power to choose—women leaders can help create vibrant, sustainable organizations.

2

The Seven Deadly Traps
for Women Leaders

Women have so much to offer, so much pure potential and talent. Yet a great deal of our skill remains untapped in organizations. What on earth is in the way? To a certain degree, we are. Unwittingly, even women leaders—we who are often described as powerhouses of strength, imagination, and creativity—often limit ourselves. We do this when we fall into any one of seven deadly traps.

1. Being One of the Boys
2. Martyrdom: "I'll Do It Myself"
3. Having No Voice and No Choice
4. Waiting for Rescue
5. Peace at Any Price
6. Hurry, Hurry, Hurry!
7. Self-protection

We are intuitively aware of certain pitfalls to avoid, knowing that we may cause great harm to ourselves by not watching out for them. Each of these traps is a pitfall, an avoidable obstacle that—if we remain conscious of it and plan accordingly—need not hinder our effectiveness and personal power. Our conscious attention, however, is paramount. For this reason, each of the seven traps is presented here in detail, to help you identify the one that holds you back. Ideally you will kick free from it, fully accessing your sovereignty as a leader.

Trap 1
Being One of the Boys

While it's true that women have increasingly asserted themselves in organizations over the past thirty years, we have made these gains somewhat tentatively. We've sensed that we were entering a territory not of our own creation. As though we had been invited into the boys' clubhouse, we believed that if we wanted to stay, we had better not disrupt the status quo. It would serve us better, we reasoned, to lie low, fit in, learn to get along. We chose to emulate the masculine way rather than take the precarious path of feminine expression.

During the 1980s, I worked for a large corporation in Los Angeles where none of the women wore dresses; pants and suits were standard attire for both men and women. It was as though all the women had adopted a masculine style of dress, and along with it a masculine style of relating to and managing others. We had disconnected from our natural ways of being for the sake of fitting in. Other corporate and organizational cultures mimicked this trend until it became widespread. By trying to squeeze into the cookie cutter shape of the male executive, many women leaders ended up feeling we had disowned our own distinct expression. We didn't believe there was space for our fully feminine selves. We believed that if we risked expressing the very real differences in our natural ways of relating and managing, we would lose respect and credibility. We would no longer be seen as valuable contributors to the organization overall.

What We Have Lost

Some of us have disconnected so entirely from our truest expression that we no longer remember what it looks like. When we become one of the boys, we disengage from our authentic selves and lose sight of our most important work: our purpose, our calling. The tragedy is that we become unable to offer our unique gifts to the organization. We live and work with some part of us quietly grieving the loss of the feminine perspective in our organization's direction, strategy, design, and focus. The loss of the feminine directly impacts the overall sustainability of the enterprise. When women are one of the boys in meetings, the feminine circumspect view, our relational perspective, and our highly intuitive and creative input are silenced as well.

Collectively, as we have traveled the path of higher productivity, we have dropped some critical values. We rarely innovate for sustainability and the long view. We hesitate to make room and time for people to come together to enjoy a lively, inventive exchange. We don't attend to the team's natural processes and relationships. All of these are natural expressions of the feminine, and in the right environment, they are what we do best.

In addition to these losses, the omission of the feminine bears a cost to the world at large, a world which has been largely male-dominated for roughly the last two thousand years. The traditional masculine approach of rugged individualism, problem-solving, and linear focus often precludes the more holistic models of collaboration and partnership. The masculine is intensely focused and directed, goal-oriented; this is not at all a bad thing. But when it veers out of balance, the masculine can become narrow and dogmatic, resulting in simplistic solutions to complex issues, with potentially far-reaching adverse implications in the long term. Allowing a predominantly masculine approach to prevail has put us out of balance globally. Ongoing religious and political wars, the decimation of our ecosystem, and systemic corruption within both church and state are costing us all dearly. Our current systems were designed from the principles of hierarchy and domination. It is time for a new design principle. In order to address these losses we need the distinct virtues of the feminine: patience for the long view, compassionate and collaborative action, and an overarching commitment to the connectedness and importance of all life. To bring the world back into balance will require the healing gifts of the feminine, and that includes all of us.

The Gifts of the Feminine

The feminine, of course, is an archetype. It is not a particular person, gender, or group; it is more like an energy. Men and women have both masculine and feminine energies at their disposal. Though one energy may be more developed and animated than the other, both exist in every one of us. Understanding the gifts of the feminine can help us collectively to increase our openness to the gifts of both energies: gifts with the power to transform organizations, teams, and communities by bringing them into balance.

The gift of the feminine is life itself. The feminine creates and gives birth; it trusts in the process of life. It is Mother Nature, moving gracefully through the powerful cycles of birth, growth, decay, and death. Mother Nature knows when a forest needs to be cleared by fire to make room for new life. She moves us faithfully into and through the signs and seasons of change.

The feminine energy promotes healing and regeneration. The feminine is radiant, nurturing, and beautiful. The feminine can also be irrational, unpredictable, wild, and chaotic—which may explain, in part, why it is often mistrusted within a masculine orientation. The feminine brings the gift of intuition, that nonlinear knowing that can effortlessly guide an ordinary circumstance to an extraordinary outcome. The feminine facilitates passionate expression and love of life.

As we are all increasingly and painfully aware, the command-and-control (masculine) model of leadership has outlived its usefulness. Slowly but surely it will be replaced by the inspire-and-collaborate model. With this imminent transformation will come the power to fundamentally reshape the world in which we live, rather than merely influencing it. It will open the door for women to lead truly. Now is not the time to hold back, women. This is the time to give it all you've got.

Finding the Courage to Offer Your Gifts

Taking a compassionate stand on behalf of your employees in a budget meeting is no small thing: it takes courage to resist the urge to act tough around your male colleagues. One must have a great deal of self-confidence to offer intuition about a process or project. It takes guts to promote patience when the rest of the team wants to rush ahead to get it done. Finding the courage to offer the gifts of the feminine is half the battle.

Kim worked for a hydro-electric utility company, a self-described "good old boys' club." To survive in that environment, most women learned to get along by being one of the boys. Acting tough was valued and encouraged. A woman who had an eye toward climbing the ladder had best not shed a tear or show weakness of any kind.

Kim hired me because she had recently been promoted and felt unsure of herself in her new role as director. She wanted a coach who would be honest and clear with her, and she wasn't confident she could find that kind of support within the organization. There were too many hidden agendas, too much turf-guarding for trust to flourish. Kim was a second generation company woman; her father had worked his whole career at this company. Kim's promotion now made her the leader of a group composed almost entirely of men, many of whom had been employees for twenty to thirty years.

At first Kim sought coaching to become a "more effective" leader (meaning "more like a man"). Gradually, however, we discerned together that Kim's most empowering course of action would be to bring the gifts of the feminine to her new position. After all, this was her native energy, her most authentic expression. It took tremendous courage for her to show up as a woman, to offer more relational strategies for bringing the team together, and to stand firm in her commitment to developing each and every one of her employees. Kim faced enormous resistance at first; one of her employees even walked out of a meeting she was leading. But the feminine is extremely good at persevering. Over the course of eighteen months, Kim fundamentally and positively impacted the lives of each and every one of her ten teammates. She offered direct and compassionate feedback, encouraged them to take risks, and fully supported them even when they failed. She reclaimed them from resignation and apathy. Her team went on to produce extraordinary results, actively assisting in several organization-wide initiatives.

One of Kim's team members described her effectiveness this way. "One of Kim's greatest achievements has been her ability to mold an experienced but somewhat eclectic group of managers into a very tight-knit team. She accomplished this by 'walking the talk'; by setting high but achievable standards; by allowing our individual creative juices to flow; by supporting our critical business needs; through genuine listening; through sound, clear, and timely communications; by using her own heart-centered coaching skills, and when appropriate, enlisting the assistance of external coaching for the purposes of team building. Consistently she weaves it all together with a reassuring balance of compassion for people and a strategic, business focus. I believe that Kim is a consummate leader who has inspired all of us to stretch our own expectations and make a difference in all that we do."

It takes courage to show up in your native feminine energy as a leader. There are so many voices in our culture insisting that it isn't a wise idea. But I encourage you to see how much more power you have when you are tapping your authentic source. I invite you to consider the gifts you intended to offer before you silenced them in an effort to fit in. How long has it been since you expressed yourself—in your leadership role—as graceful, passionate, loving, and playful?

Showing Up

We must be willing to show up fully, bringing with us all of our feminine capacities, if we intend to shift the prevailing model of leadership from command-and-control to inspire-and-collaborate. I saw a bumper sticker recently: "It's up to the women." And I believe that, in large part, this is true. The world is in desperate need of exactly what we have to offer. We have a responsibility, therefore, to show up and bring it fully to bear.

A large part of showing up involves simply remembering. Think about what you used to love, what you once dreamed about, what you originally wanted to do and be. When we are disconnected from ourselves, we are often more in touch with what we *don't* want than with what we *do* want. You don't want to work sixty-hour weeks. You don't want to have to leave your children so much, you don't want to work for a domineering boss, you don't want to do life alone. But more importantly, what *do* you want? In the next chapter, "Follow Your Passion," we will do some exploring to help you reconnect with what you love.

In addition to remembering what you're passionate about, you must be willing to trust yourself and to go the distance with yourself. You must honor and respect all of your own cycles, your ups and downs, your failings as well as your brilliance. You must be willing to see how all of these parts of you come together with an ineffable kind of perfection. Like the moon, you must be willing to be the tiny sliver as well as the full-faced brilliance. Self-love comes first, in other words. It allows you to love and contribute to others.

When you become willing and able to deeply trust your own

feminine instincts, you remain open to any and all circumstances, all possibilities, knowing that no matter what happens you will be all right. The feminine is a survivor. When you have your feet solidly on the ground in your most authentic expression, you know that any injury that comes into your life can be healed, just as new life always replaces that which passes away. Women are remarkably resilient and patient; we can expand to include so much. Forgetting these essential gifts, discounting them, or allowing them to fall into disuse—that is the trap. Being one of the boys denies your gifts. It's a costly game that prevents you from showing up as a sovereign female leader with the power of choice.

Trap 2
Martyrdom: "I'll Do It Myself"

Women excel at many things. We can juggle numerous tasks simultaneously, a skill popularly called multi-tasking. We can get in there and get just about any job done, no matter how tedious or onerous it may be. The challenge that goes with our competence is the facility with which we become martyrs, feeling overworked and underappreciated. We often fall into a state of suffering that results from believing we are the only ones who can do it right. The dictionary defines martyr as

1. One who voluntarily suffers death as the penalty of witnessing to and refusing to renounce her religion.
2. One who sacrifices her life or something of great value for the sake of principle.

A Commitment to Suffering

A martyr is one who suffers. Out of respect for the religious martyrs who suffered for a just cause and won important victories for humanity, I want to distinguish the more mundane sort of martyrdom to which I am referring. Women are traditionally trained in martyrdom, in an ongoing pattern of suffering and personal sacrifice that is not necessarily related to any higher purpose.

For centuries, we were taught that good girls made other people happy. We followed the old adage "If you don't have something nice to say, don't say anything at all." We were encouraged to play along, play it safe, and avoid making waves. Women and girls were taught not to appear too big or noisy or distracting. Our cultural training, anchored in patriarchy, has not empowered women. We learned that it was costly to speak up and speak out, to express our needs and desires directly. And so, centuries ago, we began to employ other, more acceptable means to get our needs met and maintain our good girl status. Unfortunately, many of these methods were indirect and manipulative.

If you have been trained as a martyr, you do everything yourself without asking for help. Modern-day martyrs suffer, but not always silently. You might say something like, "After all I've done for you . . ." You might offer, "No, it's fine, I will take care of it." ("It" being stay late, work on Saturday, give up some of your budget.) Your truest needs may never be articulated, assuming that you even know what they are. Dependent on others to intuit or guess your needs, as a martyr you abdicate your sovereignty. As a result, you are left feeling dissatisfied and powerless.

Saying *Yes* to Stress

Amelia is Chief Operating Officer of a large healthcare system. Her position gives her a broad scope of control, and many talented managers report to her. Yet for all her apparent power, Amelia is a martyr. She feels ultimately responsible for every outcome. She feels great when things go smoothly and guilty when they don't. She sleeps only four to five hours per night and has gained twenty pounds in one year, mostly due to stress. When her boss asks her to take on another project, Amelia always says yes. This leader suffers as she tries to figure out how to meet all her work obligations and still have a life. Amelia is a classic "I'll do it myself" woman. Her mantra is "I need more balance in my life!" but she keeps saying yes to new demands. She believes in her own skill and stamina: on some level, she believes that she actually can do it all herself. Amelia is a prime candidate for burnout, constantly suffering for the cause, as we'll see in the next section.

The Payoff of Martyrdom

There is a reason why martyrs like Amelia seldom take action to end their suffering. Martyrdom comes with a hidden payoff. The martyr gets to be right about the insensitivity, incompetence, laziness, stupidity, and selfishness of everyone else. The martyr gets to feel proud of how hard she works and how little others do by comparison. "I work sixty hours a week, doing whatever needs to be done, while *she* breezes out of the office at five o'clock on the dot, without a backward glance." It may be true; the work environment may be filled with such inequities. Being a martyr won't change these situations, however. For change to happen, you must speak up and speak out. Modern-day martyrs are committed to suffering for their cause—and the hidden cause is *being right*.

Ending Martyrdom: A Checklist
Here is a quick checklist of actions you can take, starting today, to end your own martyrdom and begin claiming your sovereignty.

○ **Ask directly for what you want and need**
Whenever you do not ask *directly* for what you need from others yet you expect them to give it to you, you are being a martyr. The primary obstacle to ending martyrdom is to figure out what you want in any given situation. After you have figured that out, then you approach someone who can do something about it and ask directly for what you want. If you complain to your friends and colleagues about needing a raise but don't mention it to your boss, your odds of getting that raise are pretty slim.

Here's how it might sound if Amelia were to ask for what she needs from her boss: a reasonable workload. "I appreciate that you have another project for me to take on and thank you for your confidence in me. However, I have more than ten priorities right now and need you to clarify which ones I can let go of in order to take on this new project." This would help Amelia to keep her workload more balanced and would convey a partnership with her boss and his priorities.

○ **Give up the right to be right**
At the heart of martyrdom lies self-righteousness. Secretly, you know that you can do things better, faster, more creatively, more

thoroughly, and in a more organized way than anyone else can. Martyrdom is a lose-lose proposition, however; it means that people around you don't have an opportunity to contribute, to support you, to make a difference. They may begin to feel powerless and impotent around you. They lose. And you lose because you really will end up doing everything yourself! I once heard someone say, "You can be right or you can have power. Very rarely can you have both." Give up the right to be right. It's just not worth the cost.

○ **Make room for people to say *no* to you**
You may avoid asking for what you want because you're afraid of hearing *no*. You don't ask because you don't want to be turned down. Consider the courage it takes to ask for a promotion you feel you've earned. Some of my female clients take months to gather the courage to ask for what they want and need. They consider all the angles and possible scenarios first. All ultimately hope for a *yes* from their boss, the board, their team, or their partners. We may experience it as a loss of power when someone tells us *no*. To avoid getting a *no* of any kind, martyrs manipulate, coerce, and lay guilt on those around them, so others will have to meet their demands. Being able to hear *no* while maintaining your strength and sense of self is the mark of a true leader.

○ **Trust that others can make powerful choices for themselves**
Martyrs fundamentally distrust the capability of others to know and articulate their own needs. Martyrs couch their communications in feigned caretaking: "I don't want to impose on him by asking for help." The subtext to this message may

be a lack of trust in others to choose wisely and prudently for themselves. You may say, "Oh, I can't ask Karen to do that, she's already so busy!" But in fact, you *can* ask Karen and trust her to respond in whatever way is appropriate for her.

Power and joy in life result from stepping out of these patterns of resentment and martyrdom. Stop doing things that you feel resentful doing. If you can't find joy in the task or project, invite someone else to help or to take it over. Resentment and martyrdom cause long-term dissatisfaction and upset, around you and within you. Because women have been trained by generations of adept martyrs, this pattern may be the toughest habit of all to break. Stay intentional, keep your head up, and watch out for the tendency to say, "I'll do it myself." Begin asking directly for help and support, and you'll be doing everyone around you a favor.

Trap 3
Having No Voice and No Choice

Women have been victimized for centuries; there's no need to list the many atrocities that women have endured. It is more relevant to come to understand the loss of power that occurs when one is a victim without choice. The very nature of the victim lies in one's profound loss of the ability to choose. A victim has no say in the decisions, outcomes, or processes that affect her life.

Powerlessness has played a very real part in women's history. Consider that only recently, in 1920, were women granted the right to vote. We are just now beginning to gain entrance to boardrooms in numbers worth mentioning. It is so astounding when a woman finally succeeds in ascending through the layers of bureaucracy that we feature her on magazine covers and talk shows, eager to hear how the feat was accomplished! Women in general are much more familiar with powerlessness than we are with wielding power in our culture and the world at large.

Profile of a Victim

Whenever we feel wronged by another and experience a resulting drop in power, we are accepting victim status. We become victims whenever something is foisted upon us, when we no longer have the right to choose. We may feel powerless around hierarchical structure changes or office relocations. When we end up with a new boss who has been hired from outside the company or transferred to our unit, we may see ourselves as victims of circumstance.

We may be a victim of our own needs and desires: we're obsessed with a bigger house or a more luxurious car. Maybe we long for a more important title, one that entails more power. We feel that we have to work to keep up with our lavish lifestyle. We have to put up with a less than joyful relationship. In this way we become slaves to whatever machine will satisfy these demands. Anytime we think we *have* to do anything, we have entered the league of victims.

As a girl, I was a victim of sexual abuse. Later, in my twenties, I worked for an abusive boss who was moody, domineering, and patronizing. Because I didn't want to lose my job, I was covert about my dissatisfaction. I badmouthed him to whoever would listen. I undermined his ideas. Mercifully, he orchestrated my layoff by closing my department. He took the bold action I didn't have the courage to take. I was a victim.

Paradoxically, I avoided women who acted like victims. I didn't like women I perceived as weak, fragile, or confused. I had chosen a path of great strength and independence, I thought; I didn't need anyone for anything. I would never have considered myself a victim. And yet, what we resist persists.

Victims Choose to Lose

For those who lead, being a victim means that everyone loses. We lose, the people who report to us lose, our whole organization loses. Our voices and our contributions get smaller and smaller, and often our resentment grows. We become unable to effect the kinds of changes that create dynamic, lively organizations. Our relationships break down, we lose touch with our hearts, we stop believing that life is good. Life doesn't work for victims.

To stop being a victim, you must know when you're playing the game. Listen to the things you say. Do you speak like a victim? Here's how victims sound:

"I would love to stay home with my children, but I have to work."

"I am not happy in my job, but I have four more years until retirement."

"I feel exhausted, but I can't slow down."

Victim status is accompanied by a sense of resignation, by a voice that says, "There's nothing I can do to change this. It's a problem that will never go away." You believe that you're stuck with whatever lies before you.

You Always Have a Choice

Full sovereignty means knowing that you *always* have a choice. No matter what has happened to you, what is happening right now, or what may happen in the future, in the present moment the choice is yours. The one thing over which you always have control is yourself. You can choose your response to anything. Pulling out of victim stance can mean doing some hard work. You may have to wrestle with yourself to overcome years of personal and cultural programming.

Recreational Complaining

Collectively, we engage in loads of complaints. You probably get an earful of complaints at work or on the train home. I call this "recreational complaining"—complaining for sport. There is no real intention to resolve the complaint. Fixing it would ruin all the fun! We tell our husbands, when they rush into fix-it-guy mode, "I just want you to listen!" But watch out! Recreational complaining drains life energy. Here's the bad news: All those things you complain about? You are a victim of them.

Take a moment to write down ten things you often complain about. Some of my own complaints are how overwhelmed I am, the dreary weather in Seattle, my children not doing their own dishes, aches and pains in my body, the apparent ingratitude of others . . . don't get me started! What are your top ten?

My Top Ten Complaints

1. _____
2. _____
3. _____
4. _____
5. _____
6. _____
7. _____
8. _____
9. _____
10. _____

In truth, there is only one kind of complaining that makes a difference: complaining for action, or more accurately, speaking out. In this scenario, you take your complaint to someone who can do something about it. If someone at work isn't pulling her load, talk to her directly. If your team is ineffective in meetings, stop and create a new format for meetings that works for all. If your boss is driving you crazy, sit down and have a chat. If you can't discover an action that will resolve the situation, be still, calm, and silent. Retain your power. Don't squander your energy and attention.

Choosing Peace

To be a sovereign leader, you must give up complaining. In some situations your ability to remain silent can be far more empowering than complaining. Late one evening, I was returning to Seattle after a long week. My flight had arrived around half past eleven at night, and the Seattle-Tacoma airport's underground train system was closed for repairs. Consequently, passengers were being transported by bus from the satellite concourses to the main terminal. A standard bus holds sixty to seventy people, and many of the flights had brought in hundreds of passengers. The result was a long, snaking line of weary travelers waiting their turn to board a bus. Complaints were flowing freely. I looked around and reasoned that this was probably the most viable solution the airport authorities could have devised. The hour grew late, and soon only equally weary airport employees remained to help herd passengers onto the buses. There was no one to whom I could have taken a complaint for action, so I chose to remain silent. It wasn't the angry, upset kind of silence, but the empowered "all is well in my world" kind of quiet. It was an empowering choice because it left me at peace. I conserved my energy, and I got home just as quickly as if I had spent my time complaining.

Speaking Out

Speaking out is different from complaining. It is a powerful action. Sometimes you must speak out about what upsets you. Things aren't working properly, or someone's actions have placed others in harm's way. You may feel misunderstood. Maybe you're passionate about resolving a long-standing social inequity. Great—if you're in a position to do so, resolve it. Just be sure that you focus your words, your energy, and your ideas toward those who can do something about your upset or perceived injustice. March on Washington, D.C. Gather others together to add mass and volume to your complaint. Voice a complaint that effects positive organizational change.

Look back now at your list of complaints and determine

what action, if any, could be taken to resolve them. If there seems to be no action, give up your complaint about the situation. The simple action of accepting what *is*, in any given situation, often brings about movement. Resistance, on the other hand, can cause circumstances to become frozen, locked up, immobile. What you resist persists. So you must either take an action or accept the situation entirely as it is. Both are empowering choices.

My top ten complaints	One positive action I could take
1. _____	_____
2. _____	_____
3. _____	_____
4. _____	_____
5. _____	_____
6. _____	_____
7. _____	_____
8. _____	_____
9. _____	_____
10. _____	_____

Reclaiming Sovereignty, the Power to Choose

If you are committed to creating a life, a career, or a relationship of your own choosing, begin now. Look for all the places in your life where you feel you have no choice and no voice. Then stop being a victim and create a life you love. Anytime you find yourself taking the stance of a victim, consider that you have a choice and can take action to impact the situation. At the minimum, you can take your leave. Alcoholics Anonymous advises its members to "keep your car keys in your hand," as a reminder that each of us *always* has a choice about where we are and whether or not we stay there. Don't keep yourself in an unhealthy situation. Make a choice that empowers you and others. Making the move from victim to wise and confident leader can empower your organization to thrive.

Trap 4
Waiting for Rescue

Several years ago, I had the sudden realization that somewhere, deep down in my bones, I had been waiting to be rescued. It's not that I was living a miserable life. It's just that "happily ever after" sounded so promising—surely I could find a shortcut to it! I kept hoping to win the lottery, thus instantly solving all my financial problems. I was waiting for the perfect job, client, partner, and office to appear on the horizon. I secretly hoped a white knight on a fine steed would whisk me off into the sunset. I'm realizing now that there are no shortcuts. Life unfolds slowly and in its own time. Lessons are learned and relearned. People don't change very quickly. Waiting for rescue is another way of abdicating your power and sovereignty.

"Someday, my prince will come . . ." Many of us grew up with fairytales in which the handsome prince comes to rescue the poor, bedraggled young maiden. He saves her from her wicked stepsisters, from the witch's curse, from a life of misery and desperation. In the end it doesn't really matter what he is saving her from, only that he comes and takes her away from it all.

Debunking the Rescue Myth

What are you waiting for? Are you waiting for that next big title or promotion that will finally show the world just how valuable you are? Are you waiting for someone at work to quit, retire, or die so you won't have to put up with him anymore? Are you waiting for your partner or spouse to make it big so financial freedom will be yours? Are you hoping that your boss, colleague, husband, sister, or friend will change, and that when they do, you will finally have your joy?

Maybe you have battled a weight problem for years and are hoping that some brilliant scientist somewhere will discover the weight-loss solution to end all weight-loss solutions so you can finally be thin. Perhaps you are waiting to move into the perfect house in the perfect neighborhood. You might be waiting to find the spiritual community or church that will anchor you in a life filled with meaning. Maybe you are waiting for the workshop or retreat that will unlock your creativity, passion, and purpose, because surely once you know your true calling . . . You may be waiting for the kids to get older or less noisy, or for more solitude so you can write, paint, rest, create, sing, or just *be*. What are your fantasies of rescue?

Succumbing to Seduction

This may sound odd, but I find that women often succumb to seduction in business. You may be seduced by money, power, recognition, admiration. When you are seduced, you make a trade. You trade your creativity for money. You trade your intuition, instincts, and clarity for security. You trade life balance for being wanted, or for being valued as an expert. You give up authentic self-expression in order to fit in and keep your job. You trade your values for someone else's. You give up your sovereignty.

Clarissa Pinkola Estes writes about this phenomenon in *Women Who Run with the Wolves*. She says we may be seduced daily by the temptation to take the easier path. She offers:

> Something inside us says, "This is hard. But look at that beautiful something-or-other over there. That gussied-up thing looks easier, finer, more compelling." So we marry the wrong person because it makes our economic lives easier. We don't take that good poem into the finer-than-fine range but leave it in its third draft instead of raking through it one more time. This expresses a simple psychological desire not to have to toil so at the basic things of creative life. The desire to have it easier is not the trap; that is something the ego desires. Ah, but the price. The price is the trap.

Living as Though This Is It

In *A Year to Live* by Steven Levine we are invited to live this year as if it were our last. Imagine that your doctor pronounces your death one year from today. Levine invites you to consider what choices you would make, where you would work, with whom you would spend your time. What would you do if you only had one year left? Contemplating this idea ends all myths of rescue and places you squarely in front of the need to make choices that will make the biggest difference in your life. It calls you to get your life in order.

Be vigilant not to be seduced by fantasies of rescue. If you ever do hop onto the horse called Rescue, away into the sunset will be whisked your creative life, your deepest passions, your unique contribution, and your truest expression of leadership. To preserve your sovereignty, stay focused on the work before you. Stop waiting for your life to turn out. Take one positive action, and then another. Stop waiting. Get a handle on your finances, your weight, your relationships, your leadership team—now. Do work that you love. Pick up that pen, that paintbrush, chisel, and saw, and build the life you've been waiting for. It will arrive much sooner than a white knight. Create your own castle, choose a fine horse, and enjoy the magical ride home.

Trap 5
Peace at Any Price

Preserving the peace at any price is another way in which women sacrifice sovereignty. We may go out of our way to please others, withhold honest feedback from those who need it, attempt to make things okay that really aren't. Pleasing others, regardless of the cost, holds us back from true power and leadership. We give up what is most important to us in order to keep the peace. This peace at any price trap is a natural outgrowth of the rules that most women learned when we were little girls.

The Sugar and Spice Rules

Rule Number One: "Be Nice" Most of us have been well trained in being nice, making other people comfortable, not rocking the boat. Being nice is hard work and it often means denying your own needs. It means that you hold your tongue when you're angry or upset. You let unspoken hurts and injuries fester inside, draining vital energy. Women leaders who follow this rule come up against an unexpected result: people don't trust them because they don't seem real. This "niceness" is often inauthentic. People see through it. They're left wondering what you *really* think and feel. Don't confuse being nice with being kind. Being nice is a kind of gooey cover. It means smiling when you feel frustrated or irritated, and using your "girly voice" when you really want to scream. Kindness, on the other hand, comes from authentic, heartfelt caring. Kindness is a true expression of generosity toward another being.

Rule Number Two: "Get Along" This rule chides you to get along with people in your life whether or not you respect them, and to pretend to agree even when you don't. It includes your behavior toward the colleague you collide with in meetings, the rude secretary, and the egotistical executive or board member. This rule bids you to do whatever it takes to get along with them all. Getting along becomes costly, though, when you swallow your feelings or comments; when you keep your true opinions, thoughts, and ideas pushed down so far that you become resentful, exhausted, or ill. All these are sure signs that you have given up something important in order to get along.

Rule Number Three: "Avoid Conflict" Many of us believe ourselves to be the peace keepers in our families, our marriages, and our organizations. You are the one, you think, who everyone else is counting on to make things better. This Sugar and Spice rule is at the heart of "peace at any price." You may fear being called bitchy if you bring up the unsavory or point out the unworkable—so you don't speak up.

The Value of Conflict

Daphne was the president of a small employee communications firm. She hired contractors to help her deliver the work to her large clients. One contractor consistently neglected to deliver on his promises. For months Daphne made apologies to her clients, covering for this contractor and working long hours to make up for his substandard work. She hesitated to confront him because she feared his reaction might make things worse. Daphne was well trained to avoid conflict. Ultimately, after months of silence, when the situation had become unbearable, she exploded. She fired the contractor and lost a colleague. How might things have gone if she had addressed the issue sooner?

Bad news doesn't get better with time. When you avoid conflict, you miss out on what everyone involved might learn from it. Conflict isn't necessary problematic; it has positive aspects. Conflict can be seen as energy that, when channeled well, can serve any project or team. When conflict is present, it generally indicates a block in the energy of a group or relationship. Your willingness to explore and to identify the obstacle can yield great results, both at work and at home. Listening to conflict allows you to see what may be blocking you from creating a better, more workable result. Conflict has much to teach.

Keeping the peace at any price also prevents you from developing the muscle to forgive, to be complete, and to let go. In this mode, you do not trust yourself to pass through conflict to a healthy resolution. You've spent so much time biting your tongue that when at last you *do* speak up, it can be like an aggressive explosion. Most women lack what has been called the habit of limited aggression, a skill that most men have perfected. We want to avoid being labeled with the traditional stereotypes we've heard applied to other women who dared to rock the boat: *bitch, nag, ball-buster.*

What Price Authenticity?

Are you willing to make room for some people to dislike you? Are you willing for some people to have negative opinions about you? Are you willing to give up a safe and comfortable life in exchange for a life of authenticity and adventure? Will you step up and be straightforward in addressing the issues that arise between yourself and others? Are you willing to tell the truth as you experience it? To make room for others to have different, sometimes diametrically opposing truths?

Truly, you cannot please everyone. To do so would be to live a washed-out life. As a leader you are bound to meet opposition in many forms. Conflict is an ever-present feature of life in the real world. You cannot tread lightly enough to avoid it; you *can* address conflicts quickly and powerfully.

Boat-Rocking Basics

When you let go of your need for peace at any price, you may need a new set of skills. I call these "boat rocking basics": ways to escape the trap of preserving peace at any price. My mentor and colleague Dick Beckhard once told me, "Figure out your own comfort zone. Then go 10 percent past it." In other words, get uncomfortable. I took his counsel to heart and applied it to my own life. I determined the edges of my own comfort zone, those places where I was nervous, anxious, or afraid. Then I took on a practice of moving 10 percent past the edge of this zone.

Ten percent isn't life threatening; it doesn't mean flirting with danger in most cases. Going 10 percent past your comfort zone simply means taking the next step, just when the little voice inside your head says, *"Don't do it!"* What you find as a result of doing this must be a bit like what the early explorers discovered: the world is not flat; you cannot sail off the edge. Instead, new self-confidence and self-respect open before you. As Eleanor Roosevelt said, "You gain strength, courage, and confidence by every experience in which you really stop to look fear in the face. . . . You must do the thing you cannot do."

1. Begin by identifying what you are afraid to do at work. What conversations have you been avoiding? What could you say that would change things?

2. Share your opinions and thoughts truthfully. Stop trying to position your words and ideas so ultra-carefully that no one is offended or upset. Speak a little more spontaneously. If you make a mistake, you can always clarify or apologize later.

3. Look for win-win solutions. What solution could you and someone else create together that would work for all parties involved? We are immensely creative: we can often find workable alternatives if we are willing to look for them.

Trap 6
Hurry, Hurry, Hurry!

We are a culture addicted to speed. For most of us, things just don't happen fast enough. Even our high-speed Internet connection is slowing us down! We see this phenomenon in our cultural penchant for immediate gratification. We want everything the day before yesterday. Information comes barreling toward you over the Internet, over radio waves, and through the printed word at a blinding rate. Remember when you used to have to go to a nice, quiet library to do research? When you wrote down observations with a pencil in a notebook? E-mail now allows you to send messages to thousands of people with a single click. Cell phones mean that you can talk in the car while waiting at the window for your fast-food lunch. It's the era of online banking and the hope of quickly turned profits. These days we can do just about anything in a hurry, and as a result we've become increasingly impatient. We don't trust the natural rhythms of life to bring us exactly what we need when we need it.

In our headlong race toward our goals, we often rush past inspiration and creativity. We don't innovate; we simply get on the treadmill and start running. We're often so busy getting from point A to point B that we have forgotten the reason for going there in the first place. This may be a familiar scenario: It occurs to me that I need something from the next room, and I quickly get up to go after it. On my way, however, I get so distracted with fifteen other thoughts that rush into my mind that, by the time I arrive at my destination, I have no idea what I got up for! Have you ever done this? We often attribute it to senility. But the truth is we're moving too fast! At times like these I make a conscious choice to slow down. I walk back into the original room, and there I find my thought, waiting patiently for me.

With all of us rushing around at work in similar fashion, it is surprising that anything gets done at all. We don't just find ourselves losing a thought or two; we forget the overarching intention of our work. We lose sight of our original purpose, our reason for being there. You may find yourself going to work simply because you have to. You no longer say, "I love my work." You don't feel inspired or uplifted by the contribution you are making. Instead, you have made your work into a kind of muted drudgery. If you are in an executive position, you seldom have any down time. All waking hours are filled with busyness. Weekends often slip away into e-mail and playing catch-up. "But," you may counter vehemently, "I made the deadline!" However: have you ever stopped to wonder why they are called *dead* lines?

Consider that the feminine way of moving through the world is not linear, project-focused, or action-oriented. The feminine can get a lot done but not necessarily in a predictable, ordered way. A woman may attend to ten different things at once, apparently scattered and unproductive. But if she's left to her own devices all the pieces come together in the end, and *voila!* another masterpiece. The feminine has periods of expansion and contraction. During expansive times you may plan, expand, strategize, implement, do, grow, buy, take on new projects, and move quickly. During times of contraction you may rest, think, reflect, slow down, consider, divest, clean out, release, detach, and integrate. Trusting these cycles means knowing that one mode of being always follows another. Don't panic when you feel the need to rest. That quiet time will be followed by a period of productivity. The challenge is to create a life and work structure that supports and honors your natural cycles. We must learn to trust this feminine process by making room for it in our organizations. Doing so may involve a radical shift in the way work gets done. It may mean letting go of the obsession with time, and the myth of control. It may mean that by shifting a *dead* line, you throw yourself a *life* line.

A recent cover of the popular business magazine *Fast Company* demanded, "Where are all the women?" Our organizations are not structured to support the ways in which women naturally work. Most have a structured schedule with a set number of hours. To be perceived as a leader and contributor to the organization and its goals, you have to arrive at work early and stay late. You have to put in face time; meaning, quite simply, that you have to show your face at work so other people can *see* you at work. But face time isn't always the most productive time.

We experience rigid agendas, project deadlines, rigid hierarchies, tangled office politics, work delegated and redelegated because no one wants to do it, and on and on. There is no down time, no time to reflect and sit quietly. Meetings are filled with nonstop chatter, positioning, arguing a point. It is frowned upon to read in your office or, God forbid, to think or meditate. One late night, a veteran CEO of the oil and gas industry settled his worn body into his executive chair and confessed, "It's not that we men are having much fun either." Another CEO summed up the problem eloquently: "We have created organizations where no one wants to be—not even the men. Joyful time is found on the weekends or after work." A sad commentary.

We must make room for both masculine and feminine ways of working in our organizations. In certain pockets throughout the world, this change is beginning. People are beginning to consider the benefits of both feminine (process-oriented) and masculine (goal-oriented) ways of working, and creating space for both styles. It is the balance of the two that makes for a rich and lively experience in our lives, at work and at home.

How do we come to trust the feminine? We learn to manage our impatience, to calm our sense of urgency. Spring comes when it's time, summer follows, then fall and winter. We cannot schedule the seasons, we cannot force them or demand their arrival. So, too, in our own lives, we must learn to relax and breathe. We must stop and be still, take time to hear something other than the constant clamor of voices, demands, and deadlines. We must learn to listen.

Trap 7
Self-Protection

You relinquish the privilege of leadership when you take leave of your true source of power and influence, abandoning your followers in the name of self-protection. This occurs when you become more concerned about staying safe than about providing clear direction and grounding for others. Consider that when you are threatened, frightened, angry, anxious, or overwhelmed, you have been thrown from your position of leadership.

Self-Protective Strategies

Self-protection in this sense doesn't mean the necessary self care that keeps you healthy and alive: that is self-preservation, the basic human instinct to survive. Unhealthy strategies of self-protection, on the other hand, keep you walled off from others. You close up and, at some level, disengage. For some, this low grade self-protection becomes a way of life.

I have shared this concept of self-protective strategies with thousands of people in organizations internationally. The work is always an eye-opener, producing breakthroughs in leadership and lives. We begin first by talking about our blind spots, those things that other people readily perceive about us, but which we don't see. For example, I may have a habit of laughing when I feel uncomfortable or getting defensive when my ideas are challenged. These are behaviors I may not be able to see until someone points them out or gives me feedback. As leaders we must work to become aware of our blind spots. Great leaders seek input and feedback from others. Without this information we get derailed. Such feedback helps us see what we have missed; it is truly invaluable.

In my workshops I often refer to being thrown: the state in which you get caught off guard, off balance, or in a reaction to something. It's like riding a horse when it bucks unexpectedly and you end up on the ground. You are literally thrown. You can also get thrown in life. Imagine that your week is going along smoothly, you've accomplished a lot, and you feel proud of yourself. Out of the blue, on a Friday afternoon, you get a call from your boss saying that your numbers are off and she wants a full report by Monday. Your weekend has just been canceled. You're angry; really pissed off. How could she be so unreasonable? Your mind races through a thousand scenarios. Your usual clarity, your ability to make informed decisions, has gone by the wayside, along with your plans to take some time off. Your boss is clearly in the wrong. You complain to your husband, your roommate, your colleagues, anyone who will listen. And you feel better, temporarily. You have engaged in a self-protective strategy called "coalition building."

Other events that might throw you could include when your colleague gets the promotion you thought you had in the bag. Or you receive an upsetting phone call from your family. All unexpected events, all unwelcome. You are thrown. You can be thrown by little things, too. Annoying telemarketing phone calls during dinner, rude drivers on the freeway, an error on a bill that must be resolved by calling customer service. Try listing five events in the past two months during which you've been thrown.

Self-protective strategies show up when you are thrown. Each of us develops these self-protective strategies at a very young age, usually between the ages of four and eight. It's as though you take a look at your life circumstances and ask yourself: "What will I have to do to survive this?" Children learn to navigate through life by watching adults, by observing what *they* do when *they* are upset, when things aren't working well for them, when they are thrown. For example, Grandma gets critical when she's tired, Dad withdraws when he's angry, Mom becomes a martyr, taking everything upon herself and suffering in silence. Thus, children receive training by watching the role models in their lives. Without questioning whether it works or whether it is the best strategy, you integrate this early training. It becomes your way of being when you are thrown.

I was well trained in sarcasm by my dad and four uncles. It seemed I had two choices: be a quick-witted and cutting master of the snappy comeback or spend my youth in tears. I chose the former. I became very good at sarcasm; over time, it became my most used self-protective strategy. All through my growing-up years and well into my twenties, I was often the life of the party, leaving people in fits of laughter. Yet like all sarcasm, my wit was always at the expense of another. Then I married a kind and gentle man. I would become thrown in social settings, uncomfortable and awkward. In an attempt to deflect my anxiety, I would offer a sarcastic comment in public about my husband and his habits. Hurt and embarrassed he would say nothing, until we got into the car to go home. Then he would offer, "That wasn't very kind." I would say, "You have no sense of humor." Ten years later, we divorced. He had grown weary of the put-downs.

We all use self-protective strategies when we are thrown. The unconscious intention behind a self-protective strategy is to get people to back off so that you will have time to think. When you are thrown, however, you *don't* think; you *react*. While you're busy reacting, you generally don't consider the ramifications of your behavior on others. Unfortunately, the use of self-protective strategies often causes long-term adverse results. Your single greatest challenge as a leader is to identify your self-protective strategies and to consider what results they are producing in the lives of others.

What Is Your SPS?

What do *you* do when you're thrown? The following are the three self-protective strategies (SPS) most often used by women. Put a check mark by the one that you see yourself using.

○ 1. Making others wrong/blaming. People often use this SPS with people in service roles or with spouses. "What an idiot," you might mutter. "What was she thinking?" "What kind of a Mickey Mouse operation is this?" Blame puts you in an artificial one-up position, making it easy to be self-righteous. It's not your problem; you had nothing to do with it. If they had designed it better, thought it through, paid attention, handled it differently, you wouldn't be saddled with all these problems.

○ 2. Self-righteousness. If you use self-righteousness as a self-protective strategy, you are sure you know a better way, the best way; sure that you are right. It's tricky to see this strategy because inherent in it is the assurance that you are not wrong. If you tend to be a control freak, the odds are that you are self-righteous. If you tend to judge others, self-righteousness is likely to be driving your judgments. If your partner says to you, "You always have to be right," then guess what? You use self-righteousness as an SPS.

○ 3. Coalition building. This is a method of self-protection in which you gather a group of people around you who will agree with you, whatever you're upset about. "Can you believe how unfair these new corporate policies are?" "Our senior leaders are a bunch of screw-ups." This is the water cooler conversation after the meeting, where negative thoughts and feelings are often revealed. Your coalition creates a safety net by joining with you. If you tell them your criticisms, it relieves your sense of responsibility to directly address the person or situation that you see as unworkable or unfair. Coalition building keeps you feeling safe when you are thrown. It's like knitting yourself a security blanket of people who agree with you.

Every adult on the planet uses self-protective strategies. To be an effective leader, you must be able to identify your blind spots so they won't derail you. Remember, these SPS behaviors are in your blind spot, meaning that others already know this about you. If you are unsure which self-protective strategies you use when you're upset, ask your family or friends to tell you. This can be a powerful form of feedback. By exposing your blind spots, you are making a conscious decision not to be bound by them any longer.

It's important to note that self-protective strategies do perform a legitimate function; at some point they helped you survive. Self-protective strategies work. They protect us and keep us safe. The problem is that your self-protective strategy may never allow you and others around you to thrive. The use of an SPS always produces a negative effect on others. It's useful to consider that the strategies we learned when we were four- to eight-years-old are simply no longer relevant in our thirties, forties, or fifties. Just as Microsoft upgrades its software, it may be time for an upgrade in your approach to upsetting situations.

Regaining Choice
People often comment, "I can see that I use these strategies and that they aren't effective, but I don't want to stop protecting

myself. What can I do instead?" The key that unlocks these patterns is *choice*. When you are thrown, you may lose your ability to choose a response. You simply react with old, out-dated patterns. What happens to others when you act self-righteously? Are they left empowered and uplifted after interacting with you? No, they feel resentful, small, and ineffective. By examining the results that you produce in others when you use self-protective strategies, you can find the motivation to stop using them. When faced with situations and people that cause you to react, as a leader you must find a way to quiet yourself long enough to choose an empowering response, one that will better serve yourself and others.

3

The First Secret:
Follow Your Passion

So much of our precious day-to-day existence seems to revolve around hard work, toil, sacrifice, and struggle. We often feel as though we can't have our joy until after we've earned it—and by then we're too tired to enjoy it! So many people work fifty weeks a year with a meager two-week vacation (if they can find the time to take it). We race from project to project, deadline to deadline, never really arriving at the place where we can breathe a sigh of completion. The contents of our e-mail inbox seems to multiply by the minute, while a steady string of voice mail collects on our office and cell phone lines, in addition to an increasingly demanding list of work projects. All of this activity means that our minds are on constant overload. Even in our spare moments, the mind won't let us rest. Before long, anxiety and fear have become our constant companions.

In my consulting work I constantly meet women who are out of balance and overwhelmed due to demanding work schedules. Enter the smorgasbord of pharmaceuticals ready to assist us in lowering our collective anxiety by chemical means, and you have a recipe for disaster. We all know that there must be a better way to live, but how? What must we change in order to create more time and energy for ourselves, our families, and our spiritual lives?

As women leaders, so much of our energy is going out, without an equal proportion of energy coming back in to fill us up again. This isn't how our powerful feminine energy was intended to be expressed. The feminine is the life-giving and nurturing force on the planet, so it just makes good sense that we must have our energy unblocked and flowing clear and strong. But that's not going to happen if we're drained.

Women who have mastered the secret of balance know that it is essential to surround themselves with what they love, with whatever it is that replenishes their energy. To do this, however, you must *know* what you love. What feeds you and returns you to yourself? Many women are surprised to find that they don't know the answer to this question. They are much more familiar with what *others* love. You know that your son loves pasta, your husband loves watching late-night television, your assistant adores white cupcakes with pink icing. Paying constant attention to the needs of others, we lose the crucial awareness of our own needs, our own center. Being a great leader means connecting deeply with what *you* love, articulating it, living it, and leading from there. Great leaders are undeniably *themselves*. And here's the deeper secret: Leaders are able to move through the world with ease because they include everything in what they love. Think of Mother Teresa, who just kept expanding her love until she quite naturally gave care to everything and everyone who crossed her path. She loved big. Such great leaders are at home everywhere they go. But you don't have to be Mother Teresa to offer the gift of yourself.

Returning to yourself, to the heart of who you are as a human being and a leader, means honing in on the basics. First, it means finding out (remembering, actually) what you love. By consulting your intuition, connecting solidly with your own clear sense of what's needed and what's next, you gain the wisdom to solve any dilemma. You find joy within yourself.

Here are two fundamental tenets to consider as you reacquaint yourself with who you are and what you love.

Know that you have wisdom within. Have absolute faith that you possess ample wisdom to solve your own dilemmas, to answer your own questions, to make your highest and best contribution in the world. Once you have this faith in place, train yourself to quiet your mind and listen deeply for this inner wisdom.

Your skills, gifts, abilities, and loves are gateways to your most authentic self. Remembering, making room for, and consciously practicing your personal gifts and interests keeps you authentically alive and able to give your best in every moment.

The Wisdom Within

Women tend to look outside themselves for answers. As a friend once said to me, "We know something is wrong with us; we just want someone to tell us what it is and how to fix it or make it go away." We seek our answers from friends, family, counselors, and religion. We secretly hope that the next self-help book we read will change us for the better. An outward focus is not a path to sovereignty and freedom. Instead, it enslaves us to the opinions and expectations of others.

It may sound too easy, this idea that all our answers are within. But truly, you needn't look any further. Finding your innate solutions and guidance does, however, mean slowing down long enough to listen. There, inside yourself, your wisdom is seated—your certainty, your convictions—in quiet repose. Think of this inner wisdom as a wise woman whose decisions are well-considered and fair, who creatively solves even the most difficult problems with ease. If you can see even a glimmer of truth in this concept, then your work becomes clear. It's a matter of finding ways to access your own particular brand of knowing.

Gateway: Finding What You Love

Clarifying what you love is critical for any woman who longs to contact her true strength as a leader. If you look to the things you love—to those people, places, and situations that make you feel most alive—you will find your purpose, patiently waiting for you to notice it. Your wise woman knows very well the secret passions that capture your heart and whisper, "Come play with me." As Barbara Sher writes in *I Could Do Anything if I Only Knew What It Was,* "I know what you should be doing. You should be doing what you love. Only love will give you the drive to stick to something until you develop your gift."

When it comes to work, the number one rule is: Follow your passion. To live and lead your own life fully empowered, you *must* do what you love. Is it any wonder that people who love their work have a much better chance of success? It doesn't take long to remember what you love, either. It has been with you all your life. As a child you did what you loved quite naturally. Back then you weren't plagued, as adults are, with a quandary about what you should or shouldn't be doing. You just did what seemed like fun. Children don't question their instincts. They know what they love and what they don't like, and they can go back and forth between the two in an instant. If you've ever had the good fortune to spend time with a four-year-old, you know how quickly this happens. Four-year-olds may do ten things they love before breakfast!

I often ask my clients to make a list of twenty things they love: things that uplift, move, and inspire them. I ask them to reflect back on what they loved as children to see if any of those activities would still make their list today. When a woman has trouble coming up with twenty things she loves, I tell her to interview the people in her life who know her well, those who can give her ideas. Your friends, husband, partner, mom, grandfather, and favorite aunt can provide hints about what you love, but you must have the final say. Here's a sample list to get you thinking.

- Walking in the leaves in the fall.
- Laughing until my cheeks hurt.
- Loving someone, seeing everything great in them.
- Baking chocolate chip cookies.
- Listening to my favorite song.
- Painting a room a fresh, new color.
- Taking a long, hot, uninterrupted bubble bath.
- Eating a great meal with good friends.
- Engaging in a great adventure (camping, hiking, skiing, traveling).

Exercise 1: Write down twenty things that you love, right now.

1. _____
2. _____
3. _____
4. _____
5. _____
6. _____
7. _____
8. _____
9. _____
10. _____
11. _____
12. _____
13. _____
14. _____
15. _____
16. _____
17. _____
18. _____
19. _____
20. _____

Keep going until you've listed at least twenty things you love doing. You're welcome to write down even more if you're on a roll! When you have finished, read through your list slowly and look for recurring themes. You may notice that several of your entries involve solitude, or nurturing people. You may notice that in general, you like solving complex problems or using your hands to create, build, and invent. What are the common themes in the things you love to do?

Your List of Twenty reveals the gateways that will bring you back home to yourself. Your challenge now becomes finding more time to enter these gateways and to follow where they lead. In the midst of a busy life, these gateways can seem like a rabbit's hole—so well camouflaged that you've forgotten where they are. To be a real leader, however, you must find these entry points to what you love and return to them regularly. Leading well, living your sovereignty, means creating a life that includes a lot of what you love. Doing this creates balance, authenticity, and aliveness because, quite simply, you begin to love your life.

Gateway: Uncovering Your Talents

The next part of our archaeological dig to recover lost instincts occurs in the area of your strengths: those skills and abilities that come naturally to you, your innate talents.

But, you may say, *I thought you were going to help me identify what I love enough to devote my life to! I already know what I'm good at.* The reason we look here is that we generally become skilled in those areas where we have natural ability. Doing so is our path of least resistance. You may be good at organizing things and people, writing, attending to details, cooking, reading, caring for others, creating a vision, spending money, being frugal, decorating, fixing things, photographing birds, solving math problems . . . You may be good at listing what other people might be good at!

You may have been taught *Don't toot your own horn!* As a result you may have squelched your memory of your own talents. Don't worry, though. They're still there. I have a good friend who has many talents; whenever someone acknowledges her for something she has done, she says, "Thank you! It's my gift!" There's power in knowing your gifts, being in touch with what you're good at, what you're offering to the world. Your creative ease in planning and designing a fundraising event might baffle and amaze your boss. Conversely, her astute way of analyzing statistics in order to improve your work environment may seem like magic to you. By offering our gifts to each other and appreciating the specific offerings that each one brings to the table, we honor ourselves and others as a part of the greater whole.

Exercise 2: Create a list of twenty things you do well
List things that come naturally and easily to you. Again, if you can't list twenty, ask the people who know you well what you're good at. They'll help you out!

1. _____
2. _____
3. _____
4. _____
5. _____
6. _____
7. _____
8. _____
9. _____
10. _____
11. _____
12. _____
13. _____
14. _____
15. _____

16. _____
17. _____
18. _____
19. _____
20. _____

Gateway: Five Other Lives

In order to claim true sovereignty over our lives, we women must leave our comfort zones and begin to think outside the box. The box is your comfort zone—cozy, maybe, but uninspiring. One of the ways to think outside the box is to allow yourself to *imagine*. What if you could live an entirely different life from the one you are now living? What would you do if you could do anything? Who would you be if you could live during any time in history, or in the future? What kind of life would you create for yourself if you could be or see or create anything at all? Think wild. Climb out of the box labeled "Reasonable and Sensible." Imagine that you could live *five different lives* totally independent of the life you are now living. You might live during any period of time: past, present, or future. You might be male, female, or even nonhuman. In each of these lives, you can be and do and have whatever your heart desires. What do those five lives look like?

This exercise is one of my favorites. It's like being five years old again, when you tirelessly invented scenarios about who you would become when you grew up—and sometimes it changed every hour! You wanted to be a fireman, then a doctor, then a bullfighter, then a mommy. Children are completely comfortable playing with ideas and dreams. They wear it all loosely, without censoring or imposing pesky reality checks.

As we get older, though, we stop allowing ourselves to be quite so playful with our dreams. We don't want to be laughed at or told that our ideas are unrealistic. We put up our guard against disappointment, and in the process we build a wall that keeps out imagination and stunts our dreams.

Here are some of the responses I've collected from female clients about the other lives they would live.

- A pioneer making my way across America, experiencing adventures, triumphs, and struggles.
- An eagle able to soar over the land, taking in beautiful vistas.
- A male photographer for *National Geographic*: no ties, no permanent home, just traveling the world.
- A well-loved house cat.

Exercise 3: Write down five other lives that you might live
Play with your list; let it be fun. For each life you would live, write down why you would want to live that life. What is it about that scenario that's compelling?

1._____

_____

2._____

_____

3._____

_____

4._____

_____

5._____

_____

You have now completed three lists: things you love, things you are good at, and five other lives of your imagining. Read through them all in sequence, and see if you can identify common themes. Some examples of themes that might arise in your lists are love of nature, love of nurturing and serving others, love of family and intimacy, love of challenge, love of discovery. Looking at all your lists together quickly is sort of like blurring your eyes to see the picture hidden in the picture.

These lists reveal the bones of what you love enough to devote your life to. This is only a skeletal outline of your ideal life; it's a sketch of what brings you joy rather than step-by-step directions about how to make your dreams take shape. For example you may see a theme of generosity, which would indicate that giving or sharing in myriad ways will bring you more of what you want in life. How, when, and with whom you will express your generosity has not yet been clarified. But you do know that being generous is an important part of who you are, it's what you love, and so you must begin looking deeply into your life to find ways of giving that are meaningful to you.

What are the themes in your life? Do you love adventure and risk-taking, or creating, or leading others to express their greatest selves, or teaching and sharing your wisdom? In my work with women, this is the point at which, together, we identify five to seven themes that capture the essence of all that a person loves. This part of our work is often the most exhilarating; it's like panning for gold, sifting through pan after pan of mud and rocks until suddenly we see a shimmering stone at the bottom. Aha! You reach for it and it is yours forever.

Once you've clarified your five to seven themes, you can begin to shape your life so it consistently reflects what you love.

What joy there is in being able to say at the close of each day, "I *love* my life!" Every day becomes a fresh opportunity to express your gifts and natural abilities at work, in your community, and in your family. By living the life that is most authentic to you, you gain sovereignty. You're a natural leader, showing the way for others. You become a living blessing.

4

The Second Secret:
Be Your Own Number One Priority

The last thing most women would want to be called is *selfish*. In fact, we often say *yes* when we mean *no*, and at times do things we resent, all in order to avoid appearing selfish. And yet, many women live on the edge of overwhelm. We are managing more complex lives than our grandmothers ever dreamt of. Like me, you probably have dozens of *must-do's* calling to you at any given moment. People want your attention; they demand your time. You have a meeting at eight in the morning, and your boss is waiting for your response to an urgent voice mail. Already the people you supervise are tapping their fingers, irritably waiting to talk to always busy and often inaccessible you. Meanwhile the pitch for your new project is coming up this afternoon and your presentation is still in a disorganized heap. You munch on a quick sandwich at your desk as you riffle through your files, fending off the people who must talk to you right away. When would you find time to take care of yourself?

Being everywhere at once, ready to answer needs, defend

your brood, or soothe conflicts at a moment's notice is the gift of the feminine—the fierce and powerful mother archetype—and we are masters at it. Yet just because you're good at it doesn't mean you should do it until you drop! It may be time to consider how you might give to yourself. Consider making self-care your number one priority. Caring for yourself is not selfish; it's critical. You must get serious about self-care if you intend to expand your best offering to the world. You cannot think clearly, make solid decisions, or stay in touch with the power of your convictions if you're worn out and exhausted. I know firsthand that this is true. I also know how challenging it can be to make changes, to work yourself into your own schedule

You regain your power and strength by taking good care of yourself; not by waiting, hoping and being resentful that no one else has stepped forward to do it. Much of true, clear leadership involves learning how to take good care of *you*. It means doing what it takes to nurture, inspire, and uplift your mind, body, and soul. There are many ways to take care of your body: by quieting your mind; through physical movement such as dance or exercise; by following your breath and focusing your attention; by setting clear boundaries; by inviting help and support; and by consciously doing things you love to do, engaging in activities that inspire you and touch your heart. Let's start with the basics: mental mastery, body awareness, full breathing, a good diet, adequate sleep, and clarity about boundaries and priorities.

The Basics of Self-Care

Master Your Mind

The more I work with leaders, the more I see the power of mental mastery, of having power and choice over your thoughts and emotions. You won't become a real leader by digging through the flotsam and jetsam of your mind. You can't think your way to authenticity and creativity. In fact, artists know they must get out of their heads to create. Yes, the mind can help you analyze problems, strategize, plan, evaluate, and rationalize. But the mind can behave like an unhousebroken puppy. You set the little tyke down on the paper, and it wanders off without your permission! You pick the puppy up, place it back on the paper, and there it goes again! Often, as soon as I sit down to be quiet, to meditate or pray, my mind reminds me of the myriad things I haven't yet attended to and demands that I get right up and get going! So often, the mind takes us down wild avenues of worry, always ready to nag about unfinished tasks.

Mastering your mind means that you choose what to place your attention on. It means consciously deciding when and where your attention goes, in spite of the demanding and arbitrary commands of your mind. Meditation helps you regain choice about which thoughts to follow, and makes you conscious of how often your thoughts cause tension in the body and limit free flow of the breath. The mind is a great ally when used with focus, but many of us let it go wherever it will. To access your intuition, the voice of your truest self, you must develop practices to quiet the mind. Only then will you hear your inner wise woman when she speaks. Only then will you be mentally strong enough to maintain sovereignty over your own life.

Return to Your Body

Masculine energy is aligned with the intellect. The feminine is more connected with the creative force of the physical body and its emotions. If you want to show up as your feminine self in the full power of your wholeness, you must care for and appreciate your physical body. Only then will you have energy for all the other things in life: that once-in-a-lifetime career opportunity; quality playtime with children, friends, and lover; writing that book that's been waiting for you to give it time and space.

Women's bodies are intuitive and wise. Your body will tell you when something is not working for you. You may get a headache or a stomachache, or feel tired. Know that these signals are trying to tell you something. Be sure to listen. Often when you're disconnected from your essential self, you're also disengaged from your body. You may not even notice you've disassociated until you reconnect through some physical experience—a close call, a sudden shock—that brings you deeply back into your body all at once. When you are disconnected, you bump into furniture, forget appointments, drop things, lose your keys. Sometimes you injure yourself physically without even realizing it. Have you ever noticed a big bruise on your leg and couldn't remember what you had run into? The body is trying to deliver an important message. The injury or pain serves two purposes. First, it wakes you up and makes you aware in the present moment. Second, an injury can help you stay present in the physical body, at least until the pain subsides. Your attention goes to the physical until the hurt is healed.

Practice paying attention to any signs that you are not at home in your body. Think of the times you neglected to eat when you were hungry, when you postponed going to the bathroom longer than you should have—times when you staved off your basic needs in favor of taking care of the needs or wishes of others. If you are habitually disconnected from your physicality, you may mask your body's signals in various ways in order to avoid acknowledging its legitimate needs. When you have a headache, you may take aspirin to quiet things down rather than listen within to find out what might have caused the pain. When you feel tired, you may drink caffeine or eat something sweet to pick you up, when you might be better off taking a break or getting some rest. To begin the journey back to yourself, notice your own physical signs of need. Be more fully present in your body.

Breathe

Many years ago, I was working full time, had two babies at home, and was halfway through a rigorous graduate program. I kept hoping that my mom would magically appear (she lived a thousand miles away) to watch the kids and cook dinner so I could get some rest, but of course she didn't. I knew that in order to keep myself going, I would have to find ways to reenergize and take care of myself. When my mother didn't come to my rescue, it forced me to realize that it was time to learn how to mother myself.

I began to notice that I held my breath a lot. Part of it was a result of holding in my stomach, which always seemed to be pooching out; but another part of it was primal and unconscious, as if I were constantly bracing myself for a blow. With all the challenges I faced as a single working mother, I felt under siege, constantly fighting for survival, and my body faithfully responded to my crisis-oriented interpretation.

Holding the breath or breathing shallowly is often a hidden source of headaches and fatigue. You may not even notice that you're not breathing. The body has a fundamental need for oxygen, however, and it's quite uncompromising about this need. To experience vibrant health and energy, you must breathe deeply through the mouth and nose. In *Eight Weeks to Optimum Health*, Dr. Andrew Weil offers a wonderful breathing practice that can be done at any time throughout the day. He invites you to notice when you are holding your breath. Then introduce a calming breathing practice: Draw your breath in to the count of seven, hold to the count of five, and breathe out to the count of eight. Do this four times and notice the difference in your well-being. Practice this simple exercise, and you will feel calmer and less tense, and your body will receive the oxygen it needs in order to perform well. As you breathe deeply, visualize releasing all the tension in your body. In this simple way, you can give your body a few moments of rest. You put your body on notice that it is not under siege, that there are no lions and tigers and bears in the immediate vicinity.

It's a tribute to our need for conscious breathing that more and more women are beginning to practice yoga poses and meditation. Both practices help you to breathe and to calm your mind. Taking the time to do conscious deep breathing can produce miracles of mental focus and overall well-being. You will be able to see complex situations more clearly and calmly. You may notice a decline in the number of headaches you experience. You will be able to contribute at a higher level as a leader. It only takes a few moments. Stop . . . and *breathe.*

Nourish Yourself

It may seem obvious, but it's important to pay attention to the quality of the fuel you put into your body. Almost every woman I know has dieted at least once in her lifetime. We are not ignorant about what it takes to stay in shape and feel good. Like a faithful engine, the body will operate only as well as the quality of fuel we give it. Fill up with the wrong type of gas, and your car may ping and sputter—the right fuel equals higher performance. Even though you understand this connection, somehow you may often ignore the relationship between what you eat and your sense of personal power and freedom. If you recognize that your diet needs to change so that you can be freer, lighter, and happier, remember that all change proceeds from awareness. The more aware you are of what you're eating—its quality or the lack thereof—the more likely you are to eat well.

A Food Diary

I began to raise my own awareness by recording, for ninety days, everything that went into my mouth. I carried a food diary, a little notebook that fit into my purse. At that time, I often forgot to eat for hours at a time, only realizing the need for food when I got a splitting headache from the drop in my blood sugar level. This habit of not eating was my downfall; I had begun to feel tired and cranky much of the time. I also drank very little water during the day, reasoning that diet cola and coffee had ample water in them. After all, my life was so busy! It seemed that I was always running to a soccer game or piano practice or a meeting. The quickest way to deal with my hunger was to eat something fast, and as is widely known, fast food is notoriously unhealthy food. Recording my food choices in my journal yielded a startling realization: the journal showed that I was eating fast food an average of eight times per week! As my awareness increased, I gradually began to make better food choices.

I invite you to begin your own food diary. For ninety days, simply write down everything you put into your body. Everything. You may be surprised at the difference between what you think you're eating and what's actually being consumed. I know from experience that anything you pay attention to is changed simply by virtue of applying your focus. The simple act of taking a good look at what you eat and drink may be enough to raise your awareness so you can make helpful changes in the way you treat your faithful body. After ninety days, or even sooner, you can begin making some new choices. As you do, you might ask yourself, "Is what I'm about to eat or drink right now going to help me raise my standard in leadership, and in life?" It's a simple change but not always an easy one. Give yourself time and keep at it.

Sleep Well

Are you getting enough rest? Do you sleep through the night? Are you sleeping too much? You need sleep to recharge your batteries. In our home, my children often came into my bedroom when they woke during the night and, too sleepy to shepherd them back to their own beds, I would move over and made room for them in mine. But I didn't sleep well with children in bed next to me. I stayed half awake, trying to make sure I didn't roll over on them, listening to their breathing for irregularities.

Sleeping with a husband or lover can make for a bad

night's sleep as well. Sleeping alongside someone else means we share energy patterns throughout the night. This is okay as long as you awake well rested. But what if you don't? In our culture, especially if you're married, there's an unspoken rule that you should sleep with your mate every night, until death do you part. Well, that day could come sooner if you don't get adequate sleep! I invite you to rewrite the rules so you can do what works. It's not an act of betrayal to sleep alone now and then. We all need deep rest. In my own case, I find that I sleep very well when I sleep alone. I find a way to do this at least a few nights a week to ensure that I'm fully rested, and it makes a big difference in my overall sense of energy and personal power. Consider what would help you ensure at least one or two nights of deep, restful sleep every week.

Raising your awareness of your lifestyle patterns by raising questions about what you are doing, both what works and what might not be working so well, is essential for taking care of yourself. You must have the basics—plenty of rest, food, water, and air—to make the kind of difference in the world that you most want to make. As the term implies, self-care requires caring about yourself. No one else can do it for you.

Create Clear Boundaries

Boundaries are made by your choices about what works for you and what won't work. Clarifying boundaries begins by knowing yourself and then becoming able to communicate to others what is and isn't acceptable, given your needs and values. The early challenge consists in identifying what isn't working for you in your life. Otherwise, how will you know what you want and don't want? If you're someone who's mystified by this question, try this simple method: pay attention to your feelings. When you're angry, upset, or frustrated, something is not working for you. A line has been crossed. A need has been ignored. I used to feel disappointed, afraid, anxious, or angry, but without the self-awareness to understand what had triggered my emotions. When my personal boundaries were crossed, I often went emotionally numb. Gradually, with practice, I learned to stay present with my emotions and to understand the areas in my life where I needed to establish clear boundaries.

The next time you get angry, stop and try to identify what it was that set you off. Was it something someone said to you, or about you? Was it an unmet need or expectation, a broken promise? Write down your findings. It may help to ask, "What do I want most right now?" Become a detective in regard to your own emotional nature. Look for the triggers. As you practice this consistent, focused exploration, you may be surprised. You may find that not only do you understand better what triggers your feelings but also you may begin to unearth your passion and creativity.

I remember when my first personal coach, Carol, told me that it was all right to set boundaries in my life. I was stunned. *Really?* I could stop answering the phone after nine at night? I could schedule myself out for lunch every day, even if I was going to be sitting at my desk with a sandwich and a magazine? I could narrow my Christmas card list from two hundred people to only those whom I really wanted to contact? There were big, scary boundaries, too. I could tell my uncle that it wasn't all right to drink alcohol at my house over the holidays? I could tell my husband not to comment on my body unless he had something loving to say? *Yes, yes,* and *yes.*

Begin by creating your list of boundaries. You don't have to share these with anyone, and even when you do, understand that your boundaries may not always be honored. But something important shifts within you as you become clear about what is and is not acceptable to you. You become strong and real.

A good friend once offered this wise counsel: "You don't have to get angry to get your needs met." You may feel angry, of course. Your anger may be covered over by sarcasm, withdrawal, or depression. You may have to wade through a fair amount of anger in order to clarify your boundaries, to find out what doesn't work for you. You may sometimes feel you have to shout at people to get what you want, but this isn't true. You have a right to simply ask for what you need from others. Eventually, as you continue to act on this truth, you will feel angry less and less of the time.

Setting boundaries is not only good for your psychological health, it also frees up your energy so you can focus on other things. Setting boundaries is a wonderful kind of self-care. It reminds you of your sovereignty: your power of choice.

Encourage Self-Sufficiency in Others
Women tend to be good caretakers: we're used to doing it all. It can feel good to be needed, to feel useful and help others. Most of us were taught to take care of others—our siblings, our parents, our grandparents—and we like to be busy. But there is some bad news about this caretaking business. We're often so busy fulfilling the needs of others that we don't take care of our own needs. Our needs often go neglected until we become sick and are forced to care for ourselves as a last resort.

When you stop caretaking other people, you help empower them with self-sufficiency. It isn't that you stop caring about people, or for them. Rather, you simply recognize that older children and adults in your life are capable of doing for themselves many of the tasks you may have been doing for them. You begin to clarify what is yours to attend to and what is none of your business.

A woman I worked with recently noticed her own caretaking pattern in the way she worked with the people who reported to her. Some even called her Mom! She considered it her responsibility to help her employees become more competent at their jobs. She spoke to them in a patronizing tone, addressing them with exaggerated patience as though they were children. Rather than empowering these people, her caretaking kept her from acknowledging that her employees were fully functioning adults and she could simply call on them to contribute at higher levels. She began to tell them, "I know you can do this and that you will find the best way." Instead of patiently (and condescendingly) showing them her way to accomplish a task, she began to encourage them to think, try, fail, and learn. Her new way of leading encourages the people around her to make their own decisions and mistakes, and, ultimately, to feel good about themselves and their work.

As a single mother, a time came when I realized I was doing the lion's share of the chores around our house. At the time, my son was twelve and my daughter eleven, yet I was still doing all of the grocery shopping, laundry, cooking, cleaning, and carpooling, plus working full time. My constant complaint was that I was overwhelmed and tired. Still, I thought of myself as a good mom. *Look at me! I can juggle so many balls in the air without dropping a single one!* The cost, however, was that I had no time to spend having fun with my kids or to enjoy a little solitude so I could recharge and rejuvenate.

When at last I realized that I had grossly underestimated my children's ability to contribute, I called a family meeting to talk about the division of labor in our little family. I began to encourage their self-sufficiency. The kids agreed to wash their own clothes and to cook several meals each month for the family. They began to feel more empowered, proud of their personal contributions. One day I overheard my son bragging to his friends, "I do all my own laundry." It was a simple change, but it had taken an enormous load off my shoulders. As a result, my kids gained greater self-sufficiency and self-esteem, and I gained time to read, write, and enjoy their company.

Does your daily schedule and workload work for you? Do you end each day energized, clear, and peaceful? If not, look around to see who might be able to help you. To whom might you delegate some responsibilities? Write down the daily, weekly, and monthly tasks you complete. Think about who else might be able do those tasks, given a little training. Find ways to delegate, delegate, delegate. Creating self-sufficiency in others will help you create a life you love. Not only that, but you'll be surprised how readily others welcome the opportunity to contribute.

Clarify Your Priorities

Every healthy organization is focused on three or four strategic initiatives at any given time. We all know that an organization that tries to implement twenty initiatives at once is following a recipe for mass insanity. Keeping three or four key initiatives in focus helps everyone to stay clear about the organization's purpose. You, too, can benefit from developing personal strategic initiatives. You might call them your *priorities*.

Observing how you are spending your time isn't always the best indication of your priorities. Some of us find that we spend very little time on what is truly important to us. Without clear priorities, you give your time away to whatever calls most loudly. You've heard the adage, "The squeaky wheel gets the grease." On any given day you are bombarded with myriad priorities, all of them marked Urgent. The list is long. You are also called, sometimes actively and sometimes indirectly or subconsciously, by social causes such as street violence, homelessness, disease, and world hunger. If you watch the evening news, listen to the radio, or read the paper, it is easy to pick out at least fifty such causes in need of urgent attention. Though it makes sense to consider where you are called to become involved and where you want to put your energies to help better the lives of others, you must be vigilant not to subjugate your own needs in the process.

Your power comes from clearly articulating your priorities and remaining true to them. If you try to attend to every cause that crosses your path, your energy can become scattered. Your challenge is to arrive at clarity about what is yours to do, and what is not yours. It is a deeply personal decision, requiring time and solitude for reflection. Although it takes some soul-searching to clarify your priorities, doing so will help you know when to say *yes* and when to say *no.*

I suggest that, like a healthy organization, you entertain no more than three or four priorities at a time. Your number one priority, remember, is to take care of yourself. Your number two, three, and four priorities should be things that you consciously choose to give your life energy to at this time. Of course your priorities will shift along with changes in your life circumstances. Your priorities may be excelling at work, buying a new house, and establishing financial security. Or, your priorities might consist of attending to friends and family, honoring obligations at work, and painting. My priorities, at this point in my life, are one, myself; two, my family; and three, my work (writing, consulting, coaching, and leading workshops). Knowing my priorities keeps my life simple. I make every choice about how to spend my time in light of these priorities.

Sometimes your priorities will make a sudden shift. Several years ago my mother was hospitalized during the Christmas holidays and had to undergo major surgery. I shifted my usual priorities so that I could spend time with my mom in the hospital. Almost overnight, Mom had become my number two priority. That's right, even in an emergency Mom was number two. I kept my self-care as number one. On leaving the hospital I would often go for a walk to get centered again, or come home and take a hot bath to rest and rejuvenate my energy. Remember, it's not selfish to always keep yourself as number one. Rather, it ensures that you'll have a deep reservoir of strength and energy to draw from when you most need it.

Priorities Practice

For forty days, allow your priorities to shape the foundation of all choices you make and all boundaries you set. Take a moment now to write down your top four priorities.

1. _____
2. _____
3. _____
4. _____

Consider how your life might look if you made yourself your own number one priority for the next forty days. We did this exercise in one of my monthly women's leadership groups. The mere concept of oneself as number one priority felt radical to many of the women in the group! One woman preferred to make her Higher Power her first priority, and herself number two. In her own way, each woman took this prioritization on as her area of focus for the upcoming month. The results were dramatic. At the next group meeting, women shared that they had increased their available energy by resting more, going to movies, getting massages, spending time with friends. One woman created the garden she had always wanted. As each woman shared, the creativity and delight in the room was palpable; there was joy and laughter in abundance. I asked them if, in the process of making themselves number one, they had neglected their families or coworkers. "Not at all!" they unanimously responded. In fact, each woman had been amazed to find that by attending to her own needs first, she had more loving energy to offer the people in her life.

Practicing self-care is one of the quickest ways of maintaining (or returning to) sanity and joy. Practicing the basics of breathing, eating well, and getting enough sleep are only the beginning. Add the less basic (but every bit as necessary) practices of boundary creation, cultivating self-sufficiency in others, and clarifying your priorities, and you are following the recipe for an extraordinary life. I challenge you to adopt these practices for a period of time and see for yourself whether they work for you. Sometimes the simple act of attending to the basics can be the catalyst for a joyful transformation!

5

The Third Secret:
Reclaim Your Power

When asked how much power they feel they have, many women leaders tell me that they feel like the real power lies in the hands of others. It seems like their bosses, their organization's senior leadership, the board of directors, or the customers they serve are holding the reins. These women leaders at times feel powerless to create more balanced work lives or to create a more humane and sustainable corporate culture. In meetings, they hesitate to bring up sensitive topics, thinking that the real power brokers run the show. A great many of these women indicate that they would welcome the opportunity to exercise more power than they currently do; they're just not sure how to go about it.

Most women aren't very good at compartmentalizing what happens in their lives: we can't shut out our concerns about our partners and children while attempting to focus on a project at work, and vice versa. The female brain in general isn't wired that way. Relationships permeate every part of our lives.

If your marriage isn't going well, it affects your life at work. If a friendship is failing, you may think about it constantly throughout the day. If your relationship with your boss is strained, you may be in a sour mood at home. Here's an often overlooked fact of leadership: the degree of power that a leader has rises in direct proportion to the quality of the relationships she has cultivated at work and beyond. Reclaiming your power, therefore, will impact the interactions you have with everyone you know. In this way, the quality of your relationships is integral to the level of energy and personal power you have at your disposal.

What makes it possible for women to have more rewarding relationships at work and at home? At the heart of great connections for women is a balance of power. The original intention of the women's movement was not to usurp men but to create a balance of power between the sexes. We don't necessarily need to have more power than others; we want equality. Having an equal say, being in healthy, cooperative partnership with those around us creates the kind of balance within which our natural powers can thrive. For us to reclaim our power, we must maintain satisfying, fulfilling relationships that express *balance*.

Creating balance in your relationships begins with understanding the basic principles of power and influence, specifically in regard to the place you occupy in your work and family systems. Many women are uncomfortable talking about power; the word itself might make you squirm. Women have so often been on the receiving end of abuses of power that you may now shy away from your innate capability to lead others and to influence outcomes. You may secretly be afraid that owning and using your personal power will turn you into a monster.

It is no surprise that in this milieu of fear, women's relationships with other women, especially work relationships, tend to get sticky from time to time. Pat Heim and Susan Murphy, coauthors of *In the Company of Women,* point out that women often work best with other women when power distinctions are absent. Heim and Murphy write of the Power Dead Even Rule, which they describe in this way:

> For a positive relationship to be possible between two women, the self-esteem and power of one must be, in the perception of each woman, similar in weight to the self-esteem and power of the other. These essential elements must be kept "dead even."

We like it best when our power is balanced—when one woman is not perceived as better than another. We thrive on a sense of cooperation, teamwork, and equal contribution. It requires no small amount of elegance and finesse to arrive at such a balance of power, but once we have accomplished it, a surge of shared energy results. In this way, power flows to women through the course and quality of their relationships much more than from the external symbols by which many men measure their personal power.

Women naturally and constantly seek this power balance within relationships with other women. If a female colleague compliments another woman (thereby increasing her power), the recipient will immediately do one of two things to rebalance the relationship. Either she will self-deprecate to decrease her perceived one-up status, or she will offer an in-kind compliment to increase the other woman's power, thus creating a match. The first scenario might go like this: "Your hair looks great." "Oh, I didn't really do anything to it." The second: "Thank you. You're so sweet." We observe the Power Dead Even Rule in all of our important female relationships because, consciously or unconsciously, we know that's what makes them work.

When women are clear about what needs to be done, the job does get done. We prefer to just get in there and get the job handled, contributing our best efforts without regard to title, position, or power. Women don't necessarily need to know who's in charge or who is boss. Consider how women work together when preparing a meal, dealing with a death, or shipping a product out the door. We work in concert. We're at our best when everyone on the team has an equal opportunity to contribute her talents toward a common goal.

If women work best in power-equal relationships, why make a distinction regarding the power of women? We must do so because, as women leaders, it behooves us to be well-versed in the overall dynamics of power—all kinds of power—in order to understand and fully engage our uniquely feminine brand of power and influence. Without the benefit of full information, we're unable to choose clearly and consciously—and the ability to make wise choices lies at the heart of great leadership. The reality is that we do work inside of a hierarchical structure where title and status have been made to matter. If you have a corner office, it says something about your relative power in the company. Office space is an external symbol of power. True power, however, is internal, it exists within. Historically, most women have operated in reaction to power rather than making choices about it from within. In order to engage and energize your full power of choice, you must understand the fundamentals of power and influence, both internal and external.

The ability to hold power with others is not as elusive as it may seem. Start by noticing how and where you lose power, how you get it back, and how you use it to serve the causes you most care about. Whatever you want to do—lead a team, participate in an important meeting, or care for a family—you need personal power and influence to accomplish it.

In my experience working with women leaders, I've noticed that, for many women, the word *power* conjures up all sorts of negative imagery: manipulation, domination, loss of control, abuse. Because women don't want to be associated with these negative traits, we erroneously conclude that power is a bad thing. As Jill Barad, former CEO of Mattel, once said, "When you apply the word *power* to a man, it means *strong and bold*—very positive attributes. When you use it to describe a woman, it suggests *bitchy, insensitive, hard.*"

True power is simply the ability to accomplish your goals, to produce results, to have influence over others. Indeed, most of us desire to have some sway over events and circumstances; that's what is needed to accomplish change. You may be trying to complete a project or to fulfill a dream, but in either case you know you can't do it alone. Margaret Mead aptly said, "Never doubt that a small group of committed citizens can change the world. Indeed, it is the only thing that ever has." Power is the ability to engage the hearts and minds of a group of committed citizens in a cause that matters. Whether that cause is a new initiative for customer service or restoring the rights of women living in Third World countries, you'll need power to make it happen.

Chances are you have had some experience with power—both with having it and with feeling powerless. To recognize the particulars of your own experience, it may be helpful to consider three power scenarios: first, loss of power in the past and the effort needed to reclaim it; second, a potential drop in power in the present and the effort needed to retain it; third, Sourcing, that is, sharing power with others as a means of creating ongoing partnership and balance. You can think of these as a series of developmental steps: first you learn to reclaim lost power, then you gain the ability to retain power, and finally you arrive at the most challenging way of being—Sourcing. It's like a pearl in process. When a grain of sand or another irritant makes its way inside an oyster, it responds to the challenge by surrounding the particle with layer after layer of iridescent mother-of-pearl. When at last the shell opens, it reveals the long-hidden beauty inside. The resulting pearl is a testament to the wisdom of nature's partnerships, a perfect image of the power of the Feminine.

Let's explore each of these three steps to full power.

Reclaiming Power from the Past

Most women leaders must do the important foundational work of reclaiming lost power from the past. Leadership requires a sturdy foundation, not one held together with bailing wire and airplane glue. As a leader, you already know that your resolve is constantly tested. As you rise in leadership, the tests become more rigorous and challenging. When this is the case, it's best to have both feet planted on solid ground.

3. Sourcing
The power and wisdom
of the Feminine opens
to reveal the pearl

2. Retaining Power
Holding what is gained,
gathering strength
and beauty

1. Reclaiming Power
The invisible inner work
that transmutes challenges

How do you know if you need to do the work of reclaiming? Here are some of the common symptoms of lost power.

○ You frequently feel drained of energy without knowing why.

○ You feel low-grade frustration, irritation, or sadness that doesn't go away.

○ You get triggered by certain personalities; for example, people who are critical or judgmental.

○ Certain issues in your life don't seem to be clearing up with time.

○ Physical symptoms persist, such as an inability to gain or lose weight, recurring illness, or frequent headaches.

○ You have been passed over for promotions or opportunities and are not sure how to change your approach to remedy the situation.

When you were a young child you were like a bowl overflowing with joy, creativity, and love. Due to life events and circumstances, certain parts of you may have gotten scattered or lost. If you were hurt in any way, you began to hide and protect your heart, your creative ideas, and your willingness to play. The hurt doesn't have to have been a big one; someone important to you may have said something hurtful without thinking and you felt crushed. You decided to be more careful next time, to protect yourself so you wouldn't get hurt again. Many of us have become so overly cautious that we forget how to be ourselves! Over time, these protective layers became thick, like a wall around your heart, mind, and energy. In a sense, those who hurt you hold power over a small piece of you, a portion of your spontaneous energy and aliveness. Of course they may not even know they have it, and you may not realize that you ever gave it away. Little by little, though, these parts of you became scattered. Your work now is to recover them so your bowl is once again overflowing; so you have full access to your joy, energy, and love. I can tell you from personal experience that this result is worth every ounce of energy it takes to reclaim your power.

You may already be feeling overwhelmed by the long list of challenges you're facing right now at work or at home. The thought of going back to dig around in your past, trying to find pieces of yourself, may seem like too much work. But there is a clear payoff for doing this important task: it can clear up a world of mischief in your present circumstances. New clarity will open up and problems will become easier to solve. Overwhelm will become a thing of the past as your intuition gains strength and clarity to guide your life choices, both big and small. Your leadership will be anchored in authenticity and creativity. Reclaiming power, therefore, is definitely worth the time it takes. Without this kind of exploration, you risk repeating the unconscious patterns of power loss again and again, until you are able and willing to see them for what they are. If you're ready for the most satisfying project of all—reclaiming yourself, your power, and your sense of aliveness—this work was made for you.

Begin by considering all the places you may have suffered a loss or decline in power. Look for this loss in past relationships with anyone toward whom you are still carrying a grudge or holding on to resentment. Your resentment may be attached to big transgressions such as abuse, betrayal, or other violations; or it may have been caused by mundane upsets, such as an unfair annual performance appraisal, a disputed promotion, criticism of your ideas in a meeting, unclear project assignments, perceived favoritism, broken promises, or a myriad of other situations that can occur at work and at home.

Exercise: Locating loss of power in the past

Look back over your past and identify any times when you felt powerless. There may be certain interactions or relationships that you still regularly think about, and which are accompanied by unpleasant feelings. Some of your most important relationships may still be strained due to past transgressions of one kind or another. The warning signs are shame, embarrassment, sadness, anger, hurt, blame, or resentment (toward another person or yourself). Write down the top three situations that occur to you, including the name of the person to whom you lost power. Hang on to this short list as you finish reading this chapter.

You will have experienced a loss of power in any situation where you were unwilling to admit your mistakes and make amends for your part in something that caused harm to someone else. You will have experienced a loss of power in any situation where you didn't claim your share of accountability, where you played the role of martyr or victim of circumstance. You will have less power concerning past situations in which you did not speak up for yourself or others, out of fear that doing so might only make things worse. We will explore each of these situations in depth, looking at what it will take to return your power and influence to its rightful place: within you.

For several years I've been sifting through the bones of my own past with the help of a counselor, a women's group, and a skilled personal coach. In this process, I noticed that I often experienced a drop in power around men, with an accompanying anxiety that didn't make sense to me. My frequent feelings of foreboding and danger often didn't come close to matching the reality of the moment. I was always on a kind of alert. In the back of my mind, I knew something bad had happened to me as a girl, but another part of me didn't want to know the specifics. "Let sleeping dogs lie" had been my general approach to any past unpleasantness in life. But my anxiety persisted.

What eventually surfaced were clear memories of abuse beginning at age four. As I moved through the healing of this abuse, I learned a lot about my own strength and stamina. I found a deep reservoir of power within myself. This knowledge now serves me well in my role as a consultant and leader, and has given me a heightened level of compassion for the suffering of others. My leadership has become clearer and more solid. I now have an intimate knowledge of what it takes to pull myself up by the bootstraps and get back into life. I challenge you to do the same for yourself.

Recently I watched a television special about the singer Tina Turner, who was involved in an abusive marriage for many years. One night after her husband had beaten her up and passed out cold, she packed her things and left. As the show's narrator put it, "She climbed up out of the wreckage of her life and began again."

One of my clients shared her own example of how power is restored to us by reclaiming the past. As the director of a large organization, she was struggling to hold on to her sense of power and contribution despite a constricting bureaucracy. Over a period of several years she had gained over fifty pounds, and I sensed that she might be feeling some resentment and resignation. (When a woman's physical appearance changes, a loss of power often lurks.)

As we looked into her not-too-distant past, she shared that several years earlier she had worked for a dominating boss who gave her very little direction and criticized her every move. Even after she was transferred to another department, her confidence remained shaken. She had lost her power and her sense of self. I encouraged her to write several letters to this former boss; not for the purpose of sending them but so she could see what she *would* say if she *could*. The first couple of letters were filled with anger and resentment. She freely accused, complained, and condemned, expressing herself fully. She burned these first letters. As she resolved things in her own heart and mind, she was able to take responsibility for her part in the relationship and to reclaim her power. The letter she actually mailed to her former boss included words of compassion and forgiveness, as well as an apology for her part in the difficult dynamics between them. She had taken responsibility for making her life whole again. By taking action in the present, this woman regained lost power from the past. In the process, she gained the intuitive understanding that forgiveness is empowering. The following year she lost over thirty pounds, as she focused on creating balance in her life and building a solid foundation of personal power.

Let's look at what you might do to reclaim lost power from your own past.

Three Strategies for Reclaiming Power

Strategy 1: Practice forgiveness; forgive all debts

We tend to hold on to hurts and resentments for a long time. We forgive, but we don't forget. Memory is long. Regarding forgiveness, my coach Sheila taught me what it means to *be complete*: she defines it as *being willing to begin anew*, no grudges, no resentments, no hanging on to old hurts. My own early training didn't prepare me well for this; I was raised in a family in which broken relationships were the norm. My father and his brother had a falling-out and didn't speak to each other for over ten years. Their example wasn't the training I needed to understand forgiveness. Sheila helped me learn how to put it into practice.

Many years ago, a colleague owed me a considerable amount of money. Time went by, and she was unable to repay me. Work was slow, every penny counted, and I really needed the money. Gradually I became resentful and angry. There seemed to be nothing I could do to change the situation; I couldn't *make* her repay me. I had lost considerable power in the situation. Hearing my ongoing complaints, Sheila suggested that I forgive the debt. At first it was inconceivable: I had *earned* that money! But as I considered the cost of my resentment and the hours I had spent in anger, I could see that no amount of money was worth it.

I called her and told her that I forgave the debt, that it was my gift to us both. As I hung up the phone, I was flooded with a peace such as I had never experienced before. She later sent me a card that I have kept all these years. It says:

Words are insufficient to express the difference your generosity has made in my life. Instantly I was moved to tears. It was as if in that moment I saw eons of humanity—past, present, and future—along with all the opportunities and openings for love between people. Forgiving that debt transformed so many cynical, resigned conversations I've had inside myself. The power of your generosity has opened doors for me that have been closed for a long time. Clearly you're doing the work, for all of us. My gratitude is not for the money, though I truly thank you. My gratitude is for what's possible for us as human beings. I want you to know that I passed on your gift by forgiving debts owed to me. It is a wise and great deed you have done.

Reading her words, I cried tears of gratitude. Now both of us were free. That is how it works: forgiveness returns power to both sides of the relationship, whether the other ever recognizes it or not. You may be thinking, "Oh, I could never forgive so-and-so for what she did! If I forgive her, she'll just assume she can get away with it again!" But you *can* forgive her. Think of it as a gift to yourself. What she does from here on out is not your problem or concern.

Who in your life might you still need to forgive? Right now, make a list of everyone against whom you are still holding a grievance or a grudge: a coworker, boss, parent, relative, old girlfriend or boyfriend, lover, teacher, spouse, ex-spouse, child. Next to each person's name, write down what he or she did—that thing you didn't think you could forgive, until now.

People I need to forgive

My first boyfriend

_____

_____

My boss at XYZ

_____

_____

_____

What do I need to forgive?

Dated my best friend in ninth grade

Promoted someone over me without explaining what I had done/not done to warrant my non-promotion

Once this list is complete (and don't be surprised if it's a long one!) you will begin to see where all your power and energy has been going. It will be clear why you may have felt drained and uninspired. One thing is certain: you cannot regain your power while you persist in blaming your parents, your former (or current) boss, or your spouse/partner for your problems. Reclaiming power means sincerely forgiving others, putting away grudges, and taking full responsibility for your own life.

I'm not suggesting that forgiveness is an easy task. It may, in fact, be the hardest thing you've ever done. Sometimes really bad things happen at the hands of people you know and trust. In such cases, forgiveness might seem like you've let them off the hook or condoned their behavior. But this isn't the case. People who commit harmful deeds are held accountable in unseen ways. Remember the saying, "What goes around, comes around." It's true. Leave punishment and retribution up to a higher power, then you'll be free to focus on your own life. If you get busy with forgiveness, an amazing thing will happen: your power, vitality, and clarity will return.

Strategy 2: Admit mistakes and make amends

Many leaders are derailed by an inability to admit mistakes. One of my favorite sayings goes, "If there is a kernel of truth in that carload of crap, admit it and get on with it." It is courageous to admit when you're in the wrong, to apologize, to do what it takes to make amends. Real leaders know the power of this skill. Do it, and you'll feel a notable surge of power and influence.

When I started working on this strategy, I began to notice how often I told lies. I was unconsciously trying to build myself up by giving the impression that I was wealthier, more competent, or more powerful than I really was. For years I did this, until a painful incident made the damage I was doing clear to me. While talking to a colleague one afternoon at a conference in Denver, I exaggerated my affiliation with a well-known leadership guru. I wanted her to be impressed by my circle of influence. After our conversation, though, I felt sick about the false impression I had given. I experienced a big drop in power, in my own heart and mind. Ashamed and embarrassed but committed to the truth (and to reclaiming my power), I called her and confessed.

Having to make that phone call was a powerful deterrent for me: I would surely think before speaking in the future. Lying, exaggerating, and pretending drains power away from authentic living. It forces you to devote enormous energy to keeping track of falsehoods, being extra vigilant. You can put that energy and power to much better use, in ways that help you maintain clear integrity. Now I admit my mistakes when I make them, and clean up my own messes.

Look into your own life to see what amends you need to make. What have you been unwilling to admit or to take responsibility for, until now? There is a reason why this action is the fifth step in the powerful twelve step recovery program. It works.

Strategy 3: Be accountable

Earlier we explored in depth the cost of being a victim. In order to reclaim your power from the past, you must be accountable for your part in anything that occurred. You must stop blaming yourself or others. Blame drains your power. Being accountable, on the other hand, puts your energy into integrity. Accountability means accepting that you played some part in creating each and every situation that has occurred in your life, even if your part was simply your lack of wisdom due to youth and naïveté.

Consider all the events in your life for which you may have avoided accountability. Think about what happened and examine your part in it. Doing this will return enormous power to you. Victims believe there was nothing they could have done in the face of external circumstances. When you have full power, you recognize that there are always a range of choices available to you. Choice equals power. Take yours back.

Retaining Power

Once you've done the challenging work of reclaiming lost power from the past, you must learn how to retain power in the face of challenging circumstances. In other words, learn to hold on to your power even when your back is against the wall. Retaining power requires a certain mindfulness: the ability to observe yourself, to stand back and watch how you respond to situations and circumstances. Being mindful is a fabulous practice for increasing your power. You cannot change what you cannot see. Once you can see an unworkable pattern of interaction, you have the power to change it.

Let's consider five strategies that you might employ in order to retain power in your current circumstances and relationships.

Five Strategies for Retaining Power

Strategy 1: Remain 100 percent accountable for all results in your life in the present

Remaining accountable in the present means that you are willing to answer for your actions, as well as for your inaction. If questions arise, if something goes wrong, consider your part in the issue. There's a clear distinction between saying, "It's not done," and saying, "I haven't finished it." The willingness to be accountable for what you do and for what you fail or refuse to do is a critical element of power and leadership.

Those who are not willing to be accountable make excuses; they blame others, the system, or themselves. They hide behind doors, computers, paperwork, busyness, and other people. They say things like *I didn't know; I wasn't there; I don't have time; It's not my job; That's just the way I am; Nobody told me; It isn't really hurting anyone;* and *I'm just following orders.* They are quick to complain and slow to act. In organizations, such lack of accountability will derail a project and sabotage the effectiveness of an entire team.

As in the strategy for reclaiming lost power, you must remain 100 percent accountable for every area of your life. You must refuse to blame others for the results you're getting. If a situation exists in your life, you must accept that you had something to do with it. Acknowledging accountability retains your power; it prevents you from falling into identification of yourself as a victim of circumstance. Being accountable, however, doesn't mean berating yourself; it's not about assigning fault. Remaining 100 percent accountable simply requires the willingness to be aware: to see and accept your part in creating every aspect of your life.

When I first begin coaching a struggling organizational team, I ask each person to identify his or her part in having created the problem or challenge. Then I invite each team member to take one positive action within their power to make things better. Regardless of the challenges you face at any given moment, there is always something you can do to improve current circumstances—one act of power you can implement—even if it's only an attitudinal shift. When you have full power available to you, a wider range of choices presents itself.

Strategy 2: Create empowering agreements at work, with family, in all relationships

In my work with women, I often ask them to list all the things they typically complain about. Here are a few of the most common complaints:

- ○ I'm not paid enough for what I do.
- ○ I'm not valued.
- ○ My husband/boss/family doesn't listen to me.
- ○ I'm overworked; I don't know how they expect me to do all of this.
- ○ My husband/kids don't help me enough.
- ○ I'm out of shape (too fat, too old, too flabby).
- ○ My boss/mother-in-law/husband/children/friends wear me out; I don't have enough energy to care for them all.
- ○ If I want it done right, I have to do it myself.

After listening to the complaints, I ask, "What agreements do you have in place?" The question is often met with silence. "What is an agreement?" someone will tentatively ask.

Most of us are familiar with a job description. This is a

kind of agreement. It is usually the first order of business when you start a new job. Your new boss articulates, in writing, the expectations he or she has of you. You agree to meet these expectations in exchange for a salary or hourly wage. If you break these agreements, it might mean you don't get to work there anymore.

There are also unspoken agreements imbedded in the culture of each team and organization. To be successful, you must learn what these agreements are and keep them, or lobby to change them. For example, your formal hours of work may be eight to four, but if you are in a management role, you may be expected to put in maximum face time. This means you really shouldn't leave until after six, and you should work on Saturdays. Anything less might give the impression that you are not 100 percent committed to your job.

When you marry, you create a foundational set of agreements for your marriage at the altar or in front of a judge. We're all familiar with the language of such agreements: To honor and uphold each other, through sickness and health, et cetera. Unfortunately, these agreements don't address how to handle disagreements about money, how to divide household chores, or how to raise the children. Most families could benefit greatly by creating written agreements about these issues and then working together to update them on a regular basis.

It is amazing how few conscious agreements most women have created at work, in their marriages, and with their children and extended family. If you haven't created powerful agreements with the people in your life, you are bound to experience a high degree of frustration and heartache. Agreements are the foundation of a life that works.

To Create Powerful Agreements
- ○ Determine what is not working.
- ○ Together, identify what will make this situation or relationship workable.
- ○ Create agreements that produce a win-win situation.
- ○ Write them down.
- ○ Regularly review to see whether all involved are keeping their agreements.
- ○ If agreements are continually broken, co-create consequences.

Strategy 3: Be real

In the 1970s and '80s many books were written for women about how to fit in at work. At that time, women were just beginning to enter the workforce in record numbers, and we didn't know the system. We had to learn rules our mothers never taught us in order to succeed. We learned to dress in business suits with little silk bowties. We imitated the way men behaved at work. In the process of fitting in, many of us sacrificed our authenticity. We became something we were not. The challenge now is to find your most authentic expression, both at work and at home: not always an easy task. Being real means knowing yourself. Consider what your passions are (see chapter 3). Give up your self-protective strategies (see chapter 2). Become quiet in meetings to check in with yourself, to find out what you really need to say and when it is best for you to remain silent.

A word about office politics: People who behave politically are not trusted. Acting politically in a given situation means that you think through the politics of who is involved, how they may react, and how to create the most positive outcome for yourself before you say or do something. You position yourself to minimize loss and risk. Being real, in contrast, means you are willing to speak and act in ways true to yourself, and then let the results unfold as they will. You tell the truth as you know it. Authentic people are trusted. They retain power and influence; additional power naturally accrues to them. Being real bypasses organizational politics.

I often feel like I am talking out of both sides of my mouth when I explain this power strategy. On the one hand, I invite you to be real. However, I also know that it isn't always prudent to say *exactly* what is on your heart and mind. You must practice patience and wisdom, exercising discrimination to know what you must say, when you must say it, and to whom it must be said. Being real doesn't take place overnight. It is the work of a lifetime.

Strategy 4: Build and retain trust with yourself and others

Building trust in relationships takes time. It takes even longer in work relationships because we tend to be more guarded with those we know less well. Trust, however, is the glue that holds teams and groups together. Without it, people experience fear and dread; they waste time in worry and in secret hallway conversations. Your job as leader is to create an atmosphere of heightened trust, and there are many ways to build it.

Although trust has many components, I will focus on only one here. Trust is increased when a leader is perceived as reliable and responsible. A leader must be counted on to do what she says she'll do (often referred to as walking the talk). Start to retain power in the present by making commitments that you can and will keep. One of my clients is Kent Thiry, CEO of DaVita, a kidney dialysis company based in El Segundo, California. Kent often uses the phrase, "Under-promise and over-deliver." He is keenly aware that trust is built when promises are kept and expectations exceeded.

People will listen to what you say, but their trust in you will be increased or diminished to the extent that you do what you say you will do. This is, quite simply, how people decide whether or not to follow you. To retain power in your present roles and circumstances, build trust through intentional commitments. Great leaders are absolute sticklers for keeping their word. Be careful about what you promise to do or not do. Make promises that you can and will keep.

Strategy 5: Speak up and speak out

In the midst of organizational change, it may be tempting to sit back and wait to see what will happen next. In reality, however, most of us don't sit back and relax at all during big changes. On the contrary, we're often distraught, worrying about what might happen, what we hope will happen, who we hope will stay or go. This is not the time to sit back; it is the time for you to clearly articulate your preferences, needs, and commitments, and to speak up for what you want. The more clarity with which you communicate, the more power you will experience in the challenging in-between time of organizational change.

Even if you feel as though you have not been able to speak up and speak out in the past, you can begin to do it now. Look at what's not working for you at work and home; see if there is anything that you need to speak up about. Are there relationships that need changing? Boundaries you need to set? As you become clearer about what works for you and what doesn't, you will empower yourself to begin speaking out. Much is being written today about the power of fierce and courageous conversations, and for good reason. Declare your boundaries. Speak up. Tell your boss, colleagues, and employees what you need from them in order to have a more satisfying experience at work. You may want more information regarding a project for which you are partly accountable, or you may need more timely updates on the status of changes. Ask for it. Your power will stay with you.

Sourcing: Sharing Power and Creating Partnership

This section of the book may stretch you; it may even confuse you, but I invite you to open your mind. Don't expect that you'll understand it all right away. When I first learned about the concept of *source* from my teacher, Sheila Peralta, I understood maybe a tenth of what she said. Part of me was covering my ears and singing "*La, la, la, la, la.*" In truth, I don't think I really wanted to fully understand what she was talking about because I knew it would mean making some big changes. Gradually though, I began to integrate the concept of *source* into my head and heart, and now it permeates my whole way of being. Sheila knew she was planting some seeds that might have a long germination period. A flower blooms when it's ready, and so will you.

Sourcing is the third stage of power. Simply put, it means to fully share power with another, to create true partnership.

To understand sourcing, I invite you to think of some common usages of the word: a battery is the source of power for a radio or flashlight, an electrical outlet is the source of power for a toaster.

Often, a woman is the source of power for her family. The family will reflect her, mirror her. Every mother I know is aware that her family carries her thumbprint. Consider the adage "When Momma ain't happy, ain't nobody happy!" If a woman comes home from work tired and crabby, it's only a matter of time before the entire family is acting grouchy, too. If she's whistling and enjoying herself immensely, her children and partner tend to follow suit. Try it at home if you don't believe me. You may be clearly aware that you are the source of life in your family. If you are well-fueled, happy, and content, the family thrives. If your needs are compromised, the needs of your family are often compromised, as well.

In the same way, an organization bears its leader's thumbprint. Your team or group is a reflection of your attitudes, preferences, priorities, and energy. If you like what you see in your team or group, this could be the best news you have heard all day. If you are frustrated or disappointed with your team, consider that it might be a reflection of a part of you that you don't want to see.

A leader's thumbprint quickly transfers onto the people she leads. Several years ago one of my clients, a national healthcare organization, was on the verge of bankruptcy. The leadership team was weak and ineffective, spread too thin. The board brought in a new CEO, Brian, who was young, bright, passionate, and energetic. Brian found many ways to encourage people to believe that the organization could be great again.

Most of the workers were resigned about the company and even embarrassed to admit they worked there. The new CEO had his work cut out for him.

Brian hired good people to help carry out his vision. He organized lively annual gatherings for the one thousand leaders in the company. Meetings were extraordinary, often surprising attendees with unexpected events, ceremonies, public acknowledgment, or humorous skits and songs. Reluctantly at first the employees gradually began to trust this new leader and his direction for their company. They began to laugh again, and found themselves playing and singing right along with him. Life was finding its way into a company that had been on the brink of death. The organization had acquired Brian's thumbprint; it had begun to reflect him in all the ways that mattered. He had demonstrated intentional leadership. As a consultant to this organization, I, too, was positively affected by Brian's leadership, vision, and commitment.

Sometimes, though, a leader's thumbprint can create the opposite effect. I was working with a group of managers in a five-day leadership development course, and we were discussing this concept of a leader's thumbprint on his or her team. A woman leader shared how the members of her team were constantly complaining. "They're always moaning about something," she explained with exasperation. We listened with empathy. As the week unfolded, this same leader had a thousand complaints of her own. The food was bad, she couldn't sleep in the hotel bed, the weather was depressing, and so on. This woman had projected her habit of complaining onto her team, and they had responded in kind.

Consider that the team you lead bears your thumbprint.

Everything around you, in fact, is in a sense a reflection of you: your preferences, your belief systems, your judgments, your highest aspirations, and what you most appreciate. You are the source. The people who show up every day in your life simply reflect you. It is courageous work to look this deeply, to see what you have created and how near or far it is from what you intended. What is missing? How are your truest priorities reflected in the team you lead, the family you are a part of, your marriage?

When Source is clear about her priorities and acts accordingly, life works for everyone. Sourcing means that you fuel life all around you: your very being, the way you are creates life. The people around you become their best and greatest selves if you look for, find, and draw out that which is great in them. Your concerns fall into the background as you generously give of yourself. Far different from being a victim with no choices, whose power is constantly drained by resentment, sourcing is supremely empowering. This power accrues by surrendering your ego to serve another, to serve a group, or to serve humanity at large. Sourcing happens, therefore, when you take your eyes off your own ego needs, your petty concerns or complaints, and intentionally move into service to another. You do not do this at the expense of your own well-being. Remember: to retain power, you must keep yourself as your number one priority; then you have the energy and deep reserves to whole-heartedly serve another.

In organizations, a leader is focused on doing what it takes to create workability for her team, her clients or customers, and other stakeholders. Workability means, simply, doing what works; looking for a win-win. Source is the sovereign ruler of her own life, but she is not focused on gratification or reward.

Nevertheless, rewards flow naturally, due to her attention to true service.

Let's take a look at what is needed to step into sourcing: sharing power and creating partnership.

Four Strategies for Sourcing

Strategy 1: Be a *Yes*

Being Source means being open and available to life and more life. It means being a Yes to what comes your way, whether you planned it or not. Even if you don't want to do it, or aren't sure how to do it, or don't know how it will turn out, you are a Yes. Being a Yes is about welcoming experiences, people, invitations, and adventure.

Being a Yes means being willing to do what you don't want to do. The fastest way to transform yourself as a leader and as a woman is to be willing to do what you don't want to do. Many of us are walking around in life only willing to do what we want. You can become childish this way, unwittingly limiting your life to a fairly narrow range of experience. For example, many people tell me they are afraid to speak in front of a group. If they were to limit themselves to what they wanted to do, they might never get up and use their voices in front of more than one or two people. When I encounter someone with this fear of public speaking, I invite her to step outside the comfort zone, to do what she doesn't want to do. I invite her to be a Yes.

One woman, a self-described shy person, stood up in a leadership seminar attended by about thirty people. To stretch her as a leader, I had invited her to share something she cared about. We were astonished at what she did next: she closed her eyes, and then she began to sing, quietly at first, then gaining more volume. In a voice as clear as a bell, wavering with emotion, she sang the most beautiful gospel song I have ever heard. When she opened her eyes, she saw tears streaming down the faces of her listeners. She had touched us all. We were moved by a gift that we could never have guessed she had to give. It was an extraordinary offering. We were all thankful that she had been a Yes in response to my request, even though she hadn't wanted to do it.

Being a Yes does not always mean saying *yes* to everything that comes your way, however. You reserve the right to say *no*, and whatever your answer, you always leave the person who asked feeling uplifted and encouraged. Imagine that someone in your organization invites you onto a new project team because she wants your unique perspective and contribution. You could say *yes* and join the team. But after careful reflection, you choose not to join the team, as it conflicts with several other commitments. Your response might be: "I really appreciate the invitation to join the team. It sounds like a great opportunity. However, due to other priorities, I can't commit to joining at this time. I'm willing to support the team with my feedback and assessment from time to time. I know the team that gathers will be just the right people to work on the project."

This kind of response speaks of what you are willing to do instead of what you aren't. It leaves people with your Yes. To determine what you are a Yes about, begin by looking at what will or won't work in your life. Then communicate in an empowered way, focusing on your Yes. Doing this, you keep your power in all relationships, guaranteed.

Strategy 2: Give up the right to be right

A wise person once said, "You can be right or you can have power. You can't have both." A leader is a leader because others are willing to follow. When you make others wrong, they are often unwilling to follow you. They may even sit down resentfully and refuse to move.

Here's the paradox: If you're right, someone else has to be wrong. It's impossible to evoke greatness in a person, project, or team if you're convinced that you're *right*, because it means the other must be wrong. People who are wrong don't tend to rise to greatness; they can't. If you want to be a power source, a leader who brings out the best in others and in yourself, you must give up your right to be right. Partnership requires that you stay open, collaborative, and trusting; that you continually work to foster mutual respect and empowerment. Such magic can't happen around you when you're committed to being right.

When you give up the right to be right, you listen to people differently. Instead of listening for what you do or don't agree with, you listen for the gold in what the other person is saying. You stop anticipating an argument or holding rigidly to your position. You soften and employ wisdom. As you open in this way, you become more flexible and adaptable. You encourage others' thoughts and ideas, and you are able to build on them. You enjoy calling out the greatness of others, you celebrate it. You are Source. When you take this stance, you'll be surprised at how quickly the people around you become smarter, faster, and more capable!

Recently I was describing my life with my two teenage children to two friends, mentioning in particular the challenges I was having with my daughter. It was typical teenage stuff, but

I'm not interested in typical; I want extraordinary. I asked for coaching from my friends, each of whom had raised two children of her own. Marnie encouraged me to give up my competence with my kids. She said she had seen me doing everything and being right around them, about the best way to keep house, the best way to get homework done, the best way to interact with friends. There was little room for the children to do anything their own way. And of course I didn't need the children to help *me*—I had it all together. My children had grown by leaps and bounds in their physical, mental, and emotional capacities, but I hadn't created any space for them to use their new abilities in our household.

Right away, I put this insight into practice. We held a family meeting in which I shared some of my concerns and asked for their input. I held open the space for them genuinely to contribute to our family, and they stepped in. As a result, I became more playful and less right. On the advice of my children, I changed my work schedule so I could spend more time with them. I stopped focusing so much on having all the answers and began focusing on having faith that together, as a family, we could sort out anything. I now listen more to what my teenagers are saying, instead of waiting anxiously for them to stop talking so I can tell them what I think. Our relationship is flourishing.

Strategy 3: Surrender your ego to serve another

People follow leaders who are committed to true service. Look at our modern-day heroes: Martin Luther King, Jr., Mother Teresa, Nelson Mandela. Their work was not about them personally; it was about the mission to which they were committed, the truths they believed in, the changes they knew would make the world a better place.

Women serve naturally. You know how good you feel when you have contributed to something important. You simply have to be mindful of those moments when what drives your actions is the ego rather than your sincere wish to serve. At these times, stop and silently surrender yourself into service. You don't do what you do to attain the corner office, for the big title, or for the corporate jewelry. Surrendering to service doesn't mean, however, that you accept work in a position that doesn't make full use of your abilities, or that you revert to serving coffee in meetings. It means remaining dedicated to serving the people and the causes you care about most deeply. You do what you do simply because it is the best and highest use of your resources. In the process of serving you may gain titles and offices and perks, but these rewards are not your central focus.

The concept of *servant leadership* has been developed by Robert Greenleaf. He describes it this way:

> The difference manifests itself in the care taken by the servant—first to make sure that other people's highest priority needs are being served. The best test, and most difficult to administer, is this: Do those served grow as persons? Do they, *while being served,* become healthier, wiser, freer, more autonomous, more likely themselves to become servants? And what is the effect on the least privileged in society? Will they benefit, or at least not be further deprived?

This is the work of the leader as Source, the leader who is committed to sharing power and creating partnership.

Strategy 4: Leave each and every person you interact with feeling empowered and appreciated

In his book *Old Dogs, New Tricks*, Warren Bennis offers this story:

> Queen Victoria had two great prime ministers, William Gladstone and Benjamin Disraeli. Someone once observed that when you had dinner with Gladstone, you came away thinking he was the wittiest, most intelligent, most charming person you had ever met. When you dined with Disraeli, you were sure *you* were the wittiest, most intelligent, most charming person ever.

This story perfectly illustrates the heart of Strategy 4. Reflect on how people feel after they have interacted with you. Do they feel empowered? Are they in good shape? Do others around you experience freedom and joy? Do you experience it yourself? If not, what can you do to change the way you interact with people? If you don't know, consider seeking feedback. You can do this informally by asking individuals, or more formally (and anonymously) through a feedback tool. Find out if there is anything you are doing that doesn't work for people. Be willing to ask what is needed to make your relationships more satisfying for everyone.

Research has shown that people are more productive and effective when they feel good about their work. Feeling good at work, in turn, often depends on feeling empowered and appreciated. During my years of consulting, I have learned that these two elements—empowerment and appreciation—are scarce resources in our organizations even though they cost nothing to give. Offer more appreciation than seems necessary. Maintaining a state of gratitude will dramatically shift your leadership into greatness.

Sourcing gives you the power to cause and create a life that you love. When you are Source, you don't have to wait for a single soul to change around you. You don't have to wait for the right job, the right partner, or the right circumstances. You don't have to wait until you have more money, time, or energy. You can begin right now. Being Source is both a privilege and a big responsibility. Take it on.

Remember! To be *Source:*
1. Be a Yes
2. Give up the right to be right
3. Surrender your ego to serve another
4. Leave each and every person you interact with empowered and appreciated

6

The Fourth Secret:
Create a Life of Adventure!

Do you leap out of bed every morning, excited to be alive? Can you hardly get to sleep at night because you don't want to miss a single moment? Are you completely happy and fulfilled in all aspects of your life? If these questions sound ludicrous or bizarre to you, read on.

Just for a moment, consider that we are all here on Earth to have a really a grand adventure, and that you are the architect of your life. What was the last adventure you created at work? In your marriage? With your family and friends? Let's fully explore this radical notion.

As you're probably well aware, most organizations today are moving beyond the command-and-control leadership model. As a people, we've outgrown the need for hierarchy's fixed delineations of authority. Following a chain of command isn't a natural expression for women; such an atmosphere does not inspire our best work. Collectively we have begun to affirm the power of collaboration, with its lively cross-fertilization of ideas. Any team or organization intent on real success—and breakthrough results—must be prepared to work together in ways that foster discovery, not simply follow old outmoded rules.

Collaboration suits women; instinctively we're good at it. It follows, then, that women leaders in particular possess skills which are critical to the success of organizations at this transitional and transformational time. Women have a penchant for collaborative relationship building, a natural ability to foster loyalty, native know-how in empowering others, and a drive for clarity of communication in listening as well as in speaking. Our challenge lies in re-imagining our current roles so we begin to see ourselves without limits. This challenge brings new adventures in creativity, new abilities to master, new experiences in which to become fluent, and a more feminine, enlivening orientation toward organizational leadership.

An adventure isn't something that happens to you; it's something you create. To concoct an adventure, you must imagine what would bring a juicier life to yourself and others. The central challenge for women leaders, then, is to create a compelling vision: one that promises an adventure of discovery for those who follow. Such a declaration is the act of a bold leader. Your most powerful vision focuses on what you most want—what you intend to create collectively and as an offering to your team, to your organization as a whole, and to the world at large.

The vision defines the leader. How large is your vision? How great is your belief in what is possible? John F. Kennedy saw United States astronauts traveling to the moon long before it was considered technologically attainable. Martin Luther

King, Jr. saw the complete eradication of racial prejudice. Mother Teresa saw a community of love, healing compassion, and service. Great leaders boldly declare the possibilities they see. By issuing their challenging goals in this way, a true leader lights the spark of adventure for others in her field of influence.

One of my clients, a leader in a call center for a utility company, defined her team's vision this way: "We are the heart and voice of our company." This vision empowered every member of her team. It helped them to remember the vital role they each play as the customer's primary contact. My client's vision demonstrated true leadership, rallying her team around the adventure of heart and voice.

Begin now to consider your vision. What adventures will you create in your time as a leader, as a woman, as a human being? Warren Bennis puts it this way:

> If you want to lead people, first get them to buy into a shared vision and then translate that vision into action. Leaders take people to a new place—and leaders draw other people to them by enrolling them in their vision. Leaders inspire and empower people; they pull, rather than push. This pull style attracts and energizes people to enroll in the vision and motivates people by bringing them to identify with the task and the goals, rather than by rewarding or punishing them.

We stand at a crucial moment in history. A large segment of humanity is moving away from simply responding to what occurs day-to-day and moving toward actively creating what we intend. Today, in unprecedented numbers, women enjoy more time, energy, and resources than our grandmothers would have dreamed possible. Every day presented our grandmothers and great-grandmothers with a host of external limitations; most of their energy was focused on issues of survival. As a twenty-first-century woman of the industrialized world, you have your own limitations, to be sure, but now, most often, these are internal obstacles and you can work with them. It is my hope that you feel a sense of urgency, a sense that women have a powerful role to play to insure a sustainable future for us all.

If you accept that you have been offered the gift of freedom—in that most of your day is blissfully free from having to think about what you will eat and wear, and how you will maintain shelter—you are free to become inspired to launch a meaningful contribution in the world. If you are a true leader, you feel a responsibility to go far beyond simply earning a paycheck and continuing your existence. You want your time, energy, and talents to make a difference. The most inspired among us not only feel this sense of urgency but also have the capacity to capture the hearts, minds, and imaginations of others. A leader does this by inviting others to believe that a more hopeful future is not only possible but absolutely essential. Such a leader shares her vision in a way that encourages others to find their place within it.

In seminars with women leaders, I often ask, "How many of you have articulated a vision for your life and/or for the organizations, groups, and teams you lead?" Surprisingly, very few respond in the affirmative. They've been so busy with day-to-day and week-to-week tasks that they have lost touch with the vision that originally inspired them to do what they do. Leadership guru Peter Drucker, author of more than thirty books on management and leadership, says that one of the central challenges facing leaders today is that they don't take the time to "think the big thoughts." Vision is never contained in daily details; it resides in the "big thoughts"—the kind of proactive strategy that moves you toward your goal with a thrilling sense of anticipation. When you are caught in reactive mode—putting out fires, responding to urgent e-mail and voice mail, answering only the most immediate demands—you rush through your days so quickly that you hardly remember how you spent your time. Do you ever wonder, if your focus remains only on the task at hand, if you haven't taken time to articulate a clear vision—the destination of your next adventure—then where on earth are you headed?

Creative Tension

To generate something new, you must feel creative tension. This generally happens when you begin to sense how much more is possible, and you become dissatisfied with the way things are now. You see something you want or need, changes that must be made, and a kind of tension gradually builds inside you. Without this tension you would be stalled, you would not create. This experience of tension, of urgency, is the difference between your current reality and your next adventure. For example, you envision $100,000 in your savings account and your current reality is that you have $5,000. There is a gap, and this gap becomes a sort of tension, like a rubber band stretched tight. If you can tolerate this tension and stay with it, your creative mind will get busy figuring out how to fill the gap. As a leader faced with a daunting challenge, you may find yourself waking up at odd hours of the night with new ideas, thoughts, and fresh approaches, as your creative mind wrestles with the chasm between the way things are now and the way they could be. When this happens, you're experiencing the profound effect of creative tension.

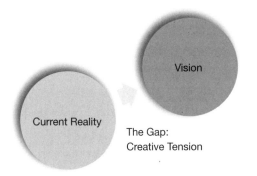

Creative Tension Model

The Creative Tension Model is adapted from the work of Robert Fritz, in his book *The Path of Least Resistance*.

The gap mentioned above is the difference between your current reality and the vision you have created for yourself and your team. The gap is creative because when you're able to stay with it, not pushing to reduce it out of frustration, anxiety, or impatience, you engage the creative capabilities of your team and yourself.

Tension always seeks resolution. To resolve the inherent tension between an invented future and the way things are right now, you have four options.

1. You can have no vision.
2. You can ignore current reality.
3. You can lower your ideals and your vision (pull your vision down closer to current reality).
4. You can take positive action to move from your current reality toward this invented future.

Let's look at each of these strategies in detail.

1. Have no vision

This is the default mode of our busy modern lifestyle. You simply react to the short-term issues and initiatives that come your way. Many people and organizations today are more opportunistic than strategic: in this mode you say yes or no to whatever comes to you instead of seeking, inventing, and creating what you intend. You worry about what you haven't yet done and how you will do more with less; you wring your hands over day-to-day employee and customer issues. The tension you experience is actually anxiety, an internal state that lowers creativity and innovation. When you have no vision of what is possible, your attention tends to lean toward what you don't want, or what you want to avoid. Some people worry about getting ill, others worry about the disapproval of their boss or getting fired from their jobs. Worriers obsess about the choices their children are making or on the possibility of personal ridicule. The list is endless. In every case, your focus is on what you do not want to happen instead of what you want to create. With this avoidance strategy, the best you can hope for is that you'll somehow head off life's disasters. You're reacting to circumstances, not creating a life.

2. Ignore your current reality

This strategy is employed in an attempt to reduce or eliminate tension. You probably would rather not see current reality in its entirety, for two reasons: First, it might make you look bad. Second, it might make others look bad. Since you may be highly invested in looking good and keeping your dirty laundry out of public view, you avoid letting anyone (least of all yourself) see how bad, difficult, or unworkable your situation actually is. You tell yourself that you should be further ahead financially, physically, emotionally; in your career, your education, your life. Rather than deal with this sense of inadequacy, you ignore it. You downplay your dissatisfaction with your current job, close your eyes to the truth of your financial situation, or disregard your body's need for rest, play, or exercise.

3. Lower your ideals

I once saw a bumper sticker that said, "If you don't like what you see, lower your standards!" If the tension of envisioning a bigger, brighter future becomes too uncomfortable, you may be tempted to settle for something that seems more within reach, more doable. You scale down your vision to bring it closer to your current reality. Instead of aspiring for your organization to be number one in customer service (which might only serve to make folks aware of just how bad the current level of service is), you might lower your standard to making a 10 percent improvement in measurable service goals over the next two years.

4. Take positive action to move from your current reality toward an invented future

Here you get going. You don't worry about how long it's taking; you just keep on. A true leader often dedicates her entire life to a single great vision. As a creative being, your imagination is always looking for some tension to resolve. You want to reach higher, be better. You want to learn to play the piano or hike through Nepal or raise amazing children. You want to build a team in which each and every member is empowered to contribute. Your creativity constantly urges you on. It's what you came here for. When your creativity is disengaged, you become bored. Life's no fun unless you're pushing the envelope, edging toward the outer limits.

Leadership means expanding your ability to stay with tension while maintaining your sanity, courage, and hope. One of my clients, a CEO for a hydro-electric utility company, has a remarkable capacity for tolerating tension. He can see the very real challenges that face the human species while holding on to his sense of optimism and hope about the changes we might make, collectively, in the world. It is a rare leader who embodies this ability.

Many of us were trained in problem-solving: see a problem, then solve it. This approach allows no pause and very little tension in between the problem and the solution. The total quality movement of the late 1980s contributed an important step in organizational evolution; it insisted that we slow down long enough to define a problem clearly and identify several viable solutions before launching into implementation. How might you slow down your process to allow for more creative tension in your leadership and in your life?

Engaging the Power of Creative Tension

Begin by clarifying objectively the current reality of your organization, your team, your family, your marriage, or your body. Tell yourself the truth about your current situation. What's working? What's not? Avoid exaggerating or minimizing your current reality. Don't color or distort your description to create an effect. Give up the need to appear good, together, wise, or normal. Here's the kicker: Only from a completely clear accounting of your current reality can you build a foundation for your future. In any area where you are unwilling or unable to see and articulate the truth of your current reality, you will also be unable to create and move toward a new adventure.

As a leader, your job is to declare and share the greatest future you can imagine. Vision has power, for in vision you can easily reach beyond the ordinary to the extraordinary. In order truly to create, you must separate what you want from what you think is possible. Our heroes did not wait until they had figured out how it could be done before they stood up to articulate a powerful vision. You may ask, "Where do I begin to create this vision?"

The following exercise originated with Pam Bartlett of Avatar Resources in Seattle, Washington. The experience is designed to be easy and to have an impact, even if you've never done anything like it before. You will need a partner whom you trust, someone with whom you can share openly.

Vision Exercise

Describe to your partner what you most want to create for your team, your organization, or your personal life. Many people find it easier to create a vision through the spoken word, rather than cloistering themselves with pen and paper. Don't worry about knowing exactly what you will say. Don't worry about making your vision perfect or complete. Start from nothing and make it up as you go.

Your partner will give you four rounds of questions. Allow three minutes to respond to each question. Ask your partner to write down what you say as you share your vision. You might even want to tape-record the session.

For **round one**, your partner will ask

What is your vision of your future five years from now?

What have you created?

What do you want?

What do you really want?

Your job is to talk for a full three minutes without stopping about what you would like to see in five years for yourself, your team, or your organization. Speak in the present tense, as though you are already living this grand adventure. For example: "I started my own company three years ago, and today we have over one hundred employees." Remember to make it exciting! Think big. Don't be reasonable; allow for limitless possibility. The creative mind loves to be unleashed and run free. Out of your wild ideas will come the seeds of a new reality, one that enlivens both you and your team.

For **round two**, have your partner ask you

What challenges did you have to overcome to make this envisioned future a reality?

Again, talk for three full minutes without stopping while your partner writes down what you say. Describe all of the obstacles you met and conquered, the fears you had to tame, the roadblocks you overcame. Talk about them all in detail.

For **round three**, have your partner ask you

What resources and people helped you along the way?

Be sure to think well beyond your current circle of people and resources. Imagine the most fabulous people helping to make your vision a reality. Share for three minutes while your partner writes down what you say. Keep going!

The **round four** question in this vision exercise is

What are you most proud of having accomplished personally?

Again, start sharing and have your partner write down your words. If it's helpful, stop a moment, get quiet and really listen to your intuition. What do you see out there, five years down the road? If you have struck gold in your vision, you may feel deeply moved by what you have helped to create. You may actually see the difference to which you have contributed. This can be a powerful experience.

At the close of the exercise, have your partner read your vision back to you. These are the seedlings of your vision. Think about them and play with them over the next few days. If you tape-recorded the session, replay it and listen for nuances. Capture what is most compelling to you. What have you helped to create in this world? Where do you see yourself in five years?

A tip: You don't have to figure out how you're going to get from where you are now to your envisioned future. Don't fall into the trap of attempting to specify the how. Author and consultant Peter Block, who pioneered the empowerment model of leadership in the early 1980s, understood that empowerment is a radical idea for organizations to embrace. To many leaders of the old guard, the concept of empowering employees seemed like giving the monkeys the keys to the zoo. Block has spoken extensively on the topic of empowerment. Again and again he was asked, "How? How? How?" His reply came in his book, *The Answer to How Is Yes.* You simply take one step, then another, then another. You say *yes*, and you get moving. The *how* will sort itself out as you go.

To move from your current reality to your envisioned future, continue to hold both images in your mind daily. Allow creative tension to work its magic. Open yourself to the possibility of chance meetings, the unexpected receipt of helpful information and gifts, and any other occurrence that moves you closer to your vision. You may find yourself doing things you have never done before, thinking thoughts you have never thought before, being moved and inspired in ways you have never experienced before. This is the creative process in action. Notice what begins to shift within you, as you move from your current reality toward the realization of your vision. All aspects of your life and leadership will realign themselves in accordance with your envisioned future. You yourself will begin to change from the inside out. Without exception, the great world leaders are those who remain open to profound change.

Robert Fritz writes, "In Martin Luther King Jr.'s early life, he experienced hatred for those who subjected black people to the injustice of racial prejudice. In his personal development, he came to embody peace and unconditional love, which changed his relationship with the situations and the people he was addressing. His nonviolent approach was only made possible by the inner strength and power resulting from the commitment to freedom and justice he embodied."

Being a hero entails giving yourself over to something

larger than yourself. To be a leader, you must lose yourself. Let go of your ego and your identity-driven needs and desires, and embrace what you are committed to creating in your organization, team, and family. True alignment with your highest purpose comes when you give up ego needs and offer your best contributions in service of the greater good. Why not create a life of adventure that serves your highest aims?

7

The Fifth Secret:
Keep Good Company

Keeping good company makes life truly delicious. The people in your life can add depth and wisdom and soul to your days, or they can distract you, drain your energy, and create upset and confusion. They can bring you to the peak of your potential and give you a clear look at your own greatness, or they can pull you down into the dark recesses of your insecurities where it's difficult to breathe. The trick is to notice that you have a say about the people with whom you spend your time and your life. You have a choice.

In your relationships you find differences that push your buttons and fuel your personal growth, and you also find the commonalities that help you feel connected. We all need friends to lean on and to support, mentors to debate with and learn from, and lovers to share our most intimate and vulnerable moments. Be deliberate about the people you gather around you. Whom do you want to learn from? Are the people in your circle those who will teach and challenge you, as well as support you and agree with you? Do they urge you to grow, or do they just make you feel comfortable?

There are two simple tests for determining whether you're in good company. First, in good company you feel free to show who you are, without fear of judgment. Second, good company encourages you to be your best self.

When you enter a new friendship or love relationship, or when you find a great mentor to guide your progress, you encounter entirely new vistas from which to observe the range of possibilities open to you. You are shaped and influenced by these close connections, by your clan. For this reason, you must choose your company wisely. In truth, what you manage to accomplish in life often has as much (and sometimes more) to do with the company you keep as it has to do with your individual efforts.

Do you surround yourself with people who call you to a higher level of leadership, life, and loving? Living with intention means that every area of your life is infused with a sense of purpose. Think about the way you go about a job or career change. You shop around carefully. Yes, the title, money, and benefits are important, but most important is whether or not the relationships and culture will provide a place where you feel you can fit in and contribute your best efforts. Most of us hope for a dream team in our new work environment. If you are fortunate, you will have an opportunity to participate in more than one extraordinary team over the span of your career. You know that you're at your best in a circle of lively collaborators who are willing to work diligently and honorably toward a remarkable goal.

The Power of Collaboration

When you have a clear sense of the people you want in your life (and the people you don't), you'll more readily make your unique contribution to your company, your community, and your family. The power of the collective is undeniable. In her groundbreaking book *The Chalice and the Blade*, Riane Eisler cites at least ten major social, educational, legal, and economic breakthroughs woman have achieved by working collaboratively: from women's suffrage to the criminalization of spousal abuse to the establishment of Women's Studies programs in universities.

The time has come for women, as a collective force, to move toward greater collaboration. As we abandon the obsolete competitive model that encouraged organizational silos, secret-keeping, and turf-guarding, we are preparing the groundwork for new levels of creative alliance and information sharing. In collaboration, parties who understand different aspects of a problem constructively explore their differences in ways that ultimately produce solutions which go well beyond the vision of any one individual. As collaborators, we reach beyond what is possible and push into the wild realm of *potential*. It's risky territory, filled with the uncertainty of new discovery. And it's a lot more fun than business as usual.

More and more is being written about collaboration, the sharing of resources, and best practices. Collaboration is effective. The good news for women is that this is the way we are wired; it's the way we work most naturally. Women are ideally positioned, therefore, to contribute in ways vital to the growth of the collaborative leadership movement.

By keeping good company, we will greatly multiply our effectiveness.

Hold Out for Your Clan

Remember the story of the ugly duckling? It turns out that she was a beautiful swan mixed up with the wrong crowd. But until she woke up to the truth, she assumed there was something terribly wrong with her. This is a common pitfall for women. You might end up in a department with a controlling manager and a group of henchmen (or henchwomen), and you soon start to feel that you just aren't tough enough to succeed. You might take assertiveness training courses and try to force your soft curves into hard, square cubicles. You suffer and strain and work, and never really have fun at any of it. If you are suffering like this, it could be a clue that you're not with your clan.

When you find yourself in a relationship or group that doesn't fit, do you immediately assume it's your fault? Women are often unwilling to say, simply, "No, thank you," and get up and leave. More often we try to bend and fold ourselves to fit uncomfortable situations that do not serve our best interests in the long run. But it doesn't have to be this way. You can watch for the signs of belonging or alienation. You can listen more faithfully to your own visceral responses to situations. You can become aware of the signs that you're not in good company, and you can notice how you feel when you're in the company of those who call you to be at your best.

You will know your clan when you see them. You will feel at home with them, at ease, even joyful. Like a swan, you will settle into the water gracefully and effortlessly. Your creativity will flow. You will feel energized and not drained. Your life direction will easily come clear. It is important to seek out your clan at work, in your friendships, and, most certainly, in your intimate relationship. Don't sell out or settle for good enough. Wait for your true clan. You will know them because in their company you feel stronger and more alive.

To find your clan, it may be necessary to leave the familiar behind. You may find yourself venturing into the unknown, letting go of old limiting alliances in favor of empowering new ones. It is often said that we undergo a major life transition about every decade of our adult lives. The transition may involve a job or career change, a major move, a health challenge, the beginning or end of a relationship, filling our nest or emptying it out. A life transition is a wonderful time to step back and evaluate the whole picture. One crucial part of that picture is the circle of people that surrounds you. You can appreciate what you have and you can consider what may be missing.

As you reflect and consider your primary relationships— your clan, your people—you may find that not all of them support and further your development as a person. You may have to let go of a few. Maybe you attracted them when you weren't clear about what you wanted, or when you were at a stage in your life which you've now outgrown. Become quiet and go within for a moment to determine who brings you life, and more life. Bless those who don't and then move on. This is what it means to keep good company. By involving yourself in clear conversations with people who reflect where you are headed in life, you hold out for your clan.

Seek Out a Teacher

There is a wonderful saying: "When the student is ready, the teacher appears." More and more women are hiring personal and professional coaches. Increasingly, organizations are developing mentoring programs, and women's networking circles are growing in number. We all can use guidance and support, no matter what our age or how long our resume. Developing a lasting relationship with a teacher insures that you continue your personal growth for a lifetime.

In my mid-thirties, I was ready for a teacher. I felt a need for additional training and development to be the leader I believed I could become. I began consciously searching for a woman, a mentor who could model the leadership skills and traits that I wanted to embody. I found Sheila Peralta. Standing all of five feet one inch, with jet black hair and solid features, Sheila had eyes of a fierce dark brown. She was simultaneously soft-hearted and tough-minded. Sheila became my coach, my partner, my role model, and my most encouraging ally.

I met Sheila in a workshop she facilitated. She was wise, light-hearted, clear, and powerful as she insisted that I break free from my own limiting tendencies. She modeled many things for me: how to stand in leadership, how to tell the truth, how to expand my integrity and accountability, how to set and keep clear boundaries in relationships, how to forgive others, how to change the patterns in my closest relationships, how to be a great mom. Sheila stood shoulder to shoulder with me through the many highs and lows I experienced during that time of quantum growth. I knew I could lean on her if needed and that she wouldn't let me fall.

One evening I was preparing to facilitate a team session with my business partner. We were experimenting with some new approaches with the team, and I was extremely nervous about failing. As I often do when frightened, I started an argument with my partner. In no time, it seemed, we were exchanging heated words; in fact, I was in tears. Rational thought had taken its leave, and I was emotionally overwrought. It was one of those times when only one thing was clear: I desperately needed a lucid voice to guide my steps.

I dialed Sheila's number. Although by now it was quite late in the evening, she answered. Crying, I was barely coherent as I wept out my fears to my teacher. Her voice was clear and insistent. "Dede, I want you to sit up straight." I did. "I want you to take a deep breath and calm down." I did exactly as she told me. "Now I want you to remember who you are: trustworthy, graceful, passionate, playful, and generous. You are a gift. The team you will work with tomorrow will be blessed by you and what you have to offer." She did not crawl down in the hole with me, nor did she sympathize with my fear and upset. She spoke to me powerfully and clearly. She was teaching me how to calm myself down and get my feet back on the ground. I have never forgotten this simple but vital lesson. With her clarity and strength, Sheila has been one of the most influential woman in my life. She is now and forever a central figure among my cohort of good company. I encourage you to find a teacher, a mentor, a coach. None of us can do it alone.

Watch Wise Women

"When seeking guidance, don't ever listen to the tiny-hearted. Be kind to them, heap them with blessing, cajole them, but do not follow their advice," writes Clarissa Pinkola Estes.

Seek out wise women. These are women who are living the same big expression of life that calls to you. Watch what they do; notice how they move in the world. Oprah Winfrey has become a wise woman to many because she is living an authentic, big life, dedicated to service and personal growth. I love to listen to the kinds of conversations Oprah encourages, the causes she supports, the people who are lifted up by virtue of having entered her circle. Oprah is living proof that women can lead with strength and with feminine flair.

Collectively, we are looking for wise women. We need more female heroes and leaders, women who know the territory of greatness. Those who preceded us have built a great fire; by its light the rest of us will find our way. We love heroes because they show us that the improbable can be accomplished, that what is difficult can be overcome. A true hero raises the bar for us all. To move to the next level of leadership, women must carefully choose our role models and heroes. We must also surround ourselves with those who can support us in becoming the heroes we are: in our family lives, in our communities, and at work. We need not only good company but great company.

Like so many others of my generation, I have had to look hard to find women leaders. There weren't many of them around to show how it was done. Even so, I knew I needed what wise women could teach. Whenever I met a woman of wisdom, I would ask her to share how she did it: How does one move in the world as a woman, fully engaged, powerful, and clear? I was burning to know. In some cases, I simply hung around these women, eagerly observing how they engaged in life. How did they interact with their children? How did they manage their time? What did they do when presented with conflicting priorities? How did they respond when they were angry or upset? What were their views on religion, politics, sex? I was hungry for their wisdom, and so I watched them.

It took a while for me to realize how these women managed to navigate so smoothly through their many roles and obligations. At first their lives looked like magic. But for them, life consistently presented only one essential task: to be powerfully and authentically who they were in every moment. By living strong as the women they were, consistent in every role and situation, these wise ones showed me the way back home to myself.

The wise women in my life have taught me how to set clear boundaries, how to say *no* when I mean it, how to raise my children with love and courage, how to take care of myself, and how to create relationships with others based on trust, integrity, and mutual respect. These wise women have helped me to learn how to be one of the girls. Now I know that this is the best gift I can possibly bring back to the world, my work, and my family: to be my authentic self.

Exercise: Consider the people in your life

Divide a piece of paper into three columns. In the first column, create a list of the people closest to you: coworkers, family members, friends, and neighbors. Then consider the predominant conversations they bring to your life. For example, if your mother is critical of you, she might initiate this kind of conversation: "Who do you think you are?" "You should really . . ." Consider each person on your list. When you think of this person, what kind of conversation immediately springs to mind? Be honest with yourself. List both the negative and the positive in the second column.

In the third column, write the great qualities of each person, the qualities you want to cultivate in yourself. Here are several examples:

Name	Conversation	Qualities
Abigail	*"You can do it! You are so great!"*	*Generous, energetic, big thinker, loving*
Margaret	*"Trust yourself, get quiet and present. You'll know exactly what to do next."*	*Strong intuition, fully present, clear, deep appreciation*
Jim	*"You're a mess. What were you thinking when you did that?"*	*None – I wouldn't want to be like Jim*

I recommend taking this exercise with you on a sabbatical; spend a minimum of five days on self-examination. No work. No business. No distractions. No newspapers. No TV. Stop and really take stock. Read through your journals. Look at your photo albums. Be still. Keep going until you have taken a full inventory of all the significant relationships in your life. Search for patterns. Then ask yourself what you might need to do to change or renew relationships with the people in your life, especially if you don't like the conversation that goes with the current relationship. You may need to end certain relationships that aren't healthy for you or decide to limit your contact with that person for a while. Keeping good company is worth all the effort it takes. Building that solid foundation of support will encourage you to show up as your best self, all the time.

Leadership involves choice and accountability. You may not always exercise choice about the characters who populate your life. Perhaps you weren't aware that you have this option. Keeping good company means that you invite people into your life who will support you in attaining your vision, those you can wholeheartedly support in return. There's a payoff to consciously choosing your clan: you will have more men and women in your life who are committed to the things that stir your heart. You will be a leader surrounded by leaders, a strong woman surrounded by strength. Collectively you will be empowered to contribute the kind of change that makes the world a better place.

A Parting Blessing

We began our journey together with a story about sovereignty in which Dame Ragnelle gained her freedom through the gift of choice. So, too, do all women gain our freedom by choice. We don't have to wait for someone else to bestow choice upon us— we can offer new choices to ourselves. If I could, I would follow you around for a few days, and at every opportunity I would say, "Choose." But since I can't do that, I'll tell you right now: Choose to do what you love. Choose to focus on what matters, what will make a difference. Choose to avoid the Seven Deadly Traps. Choose to be your own number one priority, and see what new reserves of energy you discover. Choose, daily, hourly, and moment-by-moment, to hold on to your power in any and all circumstances. Choice is your gateway to sovereignty.

Sadly, even in this age of modern life and expanded choices, we often feel powerless, as though we have no choice. Don't fall for it! You always have a choice, though the choosing itself may feel difficult or uncomfortable. Mother Teresa once said, "Profound joy of the heart is like a magnet that indicates the path of life. One has to follow it, even though one enters into a way full of difficulties." Creating an extraordinary life does not make for an easy path. But I promise you, it's worth every ounce of energy you put into it.

As women regain our power and purpose as a collective, I believe we are going to catalyze changes at a global level— changes that affect all our lives. As a woman increases her aliveness at home, her children flourish. As she steps into her power at work, reclaiming her voice and true leadership, her organization thrives. As we regain our sovereignty, our communities take heart as well, all of us growing stronger together, which in turn impacts our nation and our world in unimaginably profound and lasting ways. Always remember how important you are in the grand scheme of things. Everything you do *matters*. You can and do affect the world at large. So you must ask yourself at every turn, "Am I adding to the damage, or helping to clear it up?"

I challenge you to be Source, to accept the challenge, the auspicious responsibility, of helping restore balance to our world.

You are the one we have waited for.
Now is the time.

Recommended Resources
for Sovereign Women Leaders

The Dance of Anger: A Woman's Guide to Changing the Patterns of Intimate Relationships by Harriet Lerner. This book is one of the first I recommend to clients. It teaches how to put anger to good use in relationships.

Real Power: Stages of Personal Power in Organizations by Janet O. Hagberg. This book was among the first I read on power and it broadened my understanding immensely. Janet has developed a potent model for us all.

Loving What Is: Four Questions That Can Change Your Life by Byron Katie and Stephen Mitchell. Byron Katie calls it "doing the work," and undertaking the work at her wise direction holds out amazing discoveries. Her "turnarounds" can turn your life around in every area.

In the Company of Women: Turning Workplace Conflict into Powerful Alliances by Pat Heim, Susan Murphy, and Susan K. Golant. This is the best book I have found to teach and inspire women to work together more effectively and compassionately, with greater understanding of our inherent nature.

Waking the World: Classic Tales of Women and the Heroic Feminine by A. B. Chinen. If you like the King Arthur Story in chapter 1, Allan has many more in this wonderful book. He is doing some wonderful work on behalf of women.

The Fabric of the Future: Women Visionaries of Today Illuminate the Path to Tomorrow edited by M. J. Ryan, Patrice Wynn, and Ken Wilber. I have gone to this book again and again to expand my vision of what we women are up to as we forge our transformation, individually and collectively. The authors of this book have a passionate optimism about our future and share it with vigor.

The Power of Partnership: Seven Relationships that Will Change Your Life by Riane Eisler. After decades of groundbreaking work, Riane's latest book reveals ample evidence of her continued efforts. She outlines what it takes to create partnership in seven critical relationships, beginning with the Self.

Rebalancing the World: Why Women Belong and Men Compete and How to Restore the Ancient Equilibrium by Carol L. Flinders. I loved this book for giving a much broader context to the differences between men and women. Her work honors both.

Bibliography

Bennis, Warren. *Old Dogs, New Tricks: On Creativity and Collaboration.* Provo, Utah: Executive Excellence Publishing, 1999.

Block, Peter. *The Answer to How Is Yes: Acting on What Matters.* San Francisco: Berrett-Koehler Publishers, 2001.

Campbell, Joseph. *The Hero with a Thousand Faces.* Princeton: Princeton University Press, 1972.

Eisler, Riane. *The Chalice and the Blade: Our History, Our Future.* San Francisco: HarperSanFrancisco, 1988.

Estes, Clarissa Pinkola. *Women Who Run with the Wolves: Myths and Stories of the Wild Woman Archetype.* New York: Ballantine Books, 1996.

Fritz, Robert. *The Path of Least Resistance: Learning to Become the Creative Force in Your Own Life.* New York: Fawcett Columbine, 1989.

Greenleaf, Robert K. *Servant Leadership: A Journey into the Nature of Legitimate Power and Greatness*, New York: Paulist Press, 2002.

Heim, Pat, Murphy, Susan, and Golant, Susan K. *In the Company of Women: Turning Workplace Conflict into Powerful Alliances.* New York: Penguin Putnam, 2001.

Jacobson, Aileen. *Women in Charge: Dilemmas of Women in Authority.* New York: VanNostrand Reinhold, 1985

Koestenbaum, Peter and Block, Peter. *Freedom and Accountability at Work Applying Philosophic Insight to the Real World.* Somerset, NJ: Jossey-Bass/Pfeiffer, 2001.

Levine, Stephen. *A Year to Live: How to Live This Year as if It Were Your Last.* New York: Bell Tower Book Publishing, 1998.

Sher, Barbara, and Smith, Barbara. *I Could Do Anything if I Only Knew What It Was: How to Discover What You Really Want and How to Get It.* New York: Dell, 1995.

Useem, Michael. "The Leadership Lessons of Mount Everest." *Harvard Business Review*, Oct. 2001.

Weil, Andrew. *Eight Weeks to Optimum Health.* New York: Ballantine Books, 1998.

Index

abuse, 41–42, 96–99, 105
acceptance, 45–46
accountability, 24–25, 104, 111–13, 155
action, 7, 50, 56–57, 106, 137–39
adventure, 53, 131–44
aggression, 53
agreements, 114–15
amends, 110–11
anger, 58–59, 86–87, 104, 107
Answer to How Is Yes, The, 143
anxiety, 65–66, 86
appreciation, of others, 128–29
archetypes, 30, 78
asking for what you need, 23–24, 38–41,
    118–19
authenticity
    being one of the boys and, 29
    courage and, 35
    gaining access to, 21
    longing for, 2
    loss of, 48–49, 51
    love and, 66–67, 71
    lying and, 110–11
    price of, 53
    reclaiming power and, 103
    retaining power and, 116–17
    thoughts and, 79
    wise women and, 153
Avatar Resources, 140

balance
    cycles and, 56–58
    feminine energy and, 5, 7–8
    loss of, 48–49, 59, 65–66
    love and, 71
    martyrdom and, 37–38
    masculine energy and, 30
    power and, 96–99, 106
    restoring, 158
Barad, Jill, 99
Bartlett, Pam, 140
Beckhard, Dick, 53
being thrown, 59–62
Bennis, Warren, 128, 133
blame, 17, 61, 104, 110–13
blessings, 4, 76, 157–58
blind spots, 59, 63
Block, Peter, 142–43

boat-rocking, 53–54
body, 80–85
boundaries, 85–87, 153
box, thinking outside, 73
boys, being one of the, 2, 7
    Trap 1, 28–35
breathing, 81–82
burn-out, 7–8, 37, 66
busyness, 55–58, 65, 77, 135, 155

Campbell, Joseph, 19–20
caretaking, 87–89
Chalice and the Blade, The, 147
change
    global, 155, 157–58
    organizational, 17–18, 25
    Sourcing and, 129
    transformational, 9, 30–31, 92–93, 120–21,
        132–33
    vision and, 143
children, 60–61, 68–69, 73, 102, 125–26, 153
choice
    accountability and, 25, 111–13
    authenticity and, 17–18
    freedom and, 19–20, 157
    good company and, 155
    power and, 40–47
    rescue fantasy and, 49–50
    self-awareness and, 3–4
    self-protection and, 63–64
clan, 21, 146, 148–49, 155
clothing, 28–29
coaching, 32–33, 86, 104, 107–8, 114, 150–51
coalition building, 60, 62–63
collaboration, 30–31, 125, 131–34, 147
comfort zone, 53–54, 73
command-and-control, 31, 131
communication, 118–19, 124, 132
commitments, 117–18
company, good, 145–55
compartmentalization, 95
compassion, 4, 6, 30, 106
competition, 7, 147
complaining, 24–25, 43–47, 60, 114, 121
conditioning, 19
conflict, 51–53
conversations, 119, 149, 155
cooperation, 97–98

courage, 31–33, 39
creative tension, 135–43
creativity
    choice and, 46–47, 49–50
    collaboration and, 132
    good company and, 148
    limitation and, 23
    loss of, 48–49, 55
    reclaiming power and, 103
    setting boundaries and, 86
    thoughts and, 79
    vision and, 133–34, 139–40, 143, 157
    win-win solutions and, 54
credibility, 28–29
cycles, 34, 56–58

Dame Ragnelle, 14–17
DaVita Company, 118
deadlines, 57
defensiveness, 22–24
depression, 87
diet, 83–84
Disraeli, Benjamin, 128
domination, 30
dreams, 34, 73–75, 99
Drucker, Peter, 135

ego, 126, 144
Eight Weeks to Optimum Health, 82
Eisler, Riane, 147
emotions, 80, 85–87
empowerment, 87–89, 124–25, 128, 132,
    142–43, 149, 155
energy
    balanced, 58
    of conflict, 52
    feminine, 6–9, 30–31, 33
    forgiveness and, 110
    good company and, 149
    loss of, 66
    masculine, 6–9
    reclaiming power and, 111
    setting boundaries and, 87
    setting priorities and, 92
    sourcing and, 122
enthusiasm, 21
equality, 96–98
Estes, Clarissa Pinkola, 49, 152
exercises
    consider the people in your life, 153–55
    five other lives, 73–74
    forgiveness, 108–10
    list of boundaries, 86–87
    locating loss of power in the past, 104
    priorities practice, 91–92
    twenty things you do well, 72–73
    twenty things you love, 69–71
    vision exercise, 140–42

face time, 57, 115
Fast Company, 57
fear, 19, 53–54, 58–59, 65, 86, 104, 150–51
feedback, 59, 63, 128
feelings, 85–87
feminism, 5, 18, 96
fluidity, 7
focus, 6–7, 67–68
food, 83–84
forgiveness, 52, 107–10
freedom, 19–20, 23, 128, 134, 157
Freedom and Accountability at Work, 25
Fritz, Robert, 136, 143

gateways
    finding what you love, 68–71
    five other lives, 73–75
    uncovering your talents, 71–73
generosity, 75, 122
getting along, 51
gifts, of feminine, 22, 29–35, 67, 72, 108, 153
Gladstone, William, 128
global balance, 30
global change, 155, 157–58
good company, 145–55
gratification, immediate, 55
gratitude, 108, 129
Greenleaf, Robert, 127

healing, 30
Heim, Pat, 97
heroes, 19–20, 22, 140, 143–44, 152
holistic models, 30
hurrying, Trap 6, 55–58

I Could Do Anything if I Only Knew What It Was, 68
imagination, 73–74
individualism, 30
injuries, 80
inside-out reform, 18–19, 143
inspiration, 55, 78, 134
inspire-and-collaborate, 31
intention, 146
internal walls, 22–24
In the Company of Women, 97
intuition, 31, 67, 80, 103

joy
    authenticity and, 21
    following your, 157
    lack of, 57–58, 65
    love and, 67
    recovering, 75–76
    relationships and, 128
    self-awareness and, 4
    setting priorities and, 92

Kennedy, John F., 132
kindness, 51, 61
King, Martin Luther, Jr, 126, 132–33, 143
King Arthur, 11–15
Koestenbaum, Peter, 25

laughter, 21, 92, 121
Levine, Steven, 49
life transitions, 149
linear focus, 30
List of Twenty, 69–71
lives, living other, 73–74
love, 4, 66–68, 129
lying, 110–11

management, women in, 5, 40–41
    authenticity and, 114–15
    courage and, 31–33
    cycles and, 56–57
    feminine expression and, 28–29
    martyrdom and, 37
    self-doubt and, 23–24
Mandela, Nelson, 126
manipulation, 36, 39–40, 99
martyrdom, 20, 24–25, 104
    Trap 2, 35–40
Mattel, 99
Mead, Margaret, 99
media, 55, 155
meditation, 79, 82
mentors, 23–24, 145–46, 150–51
mind, mastery of, 79
mindfulness, 112
mistakes, admitting, 110–11
money, 23, 107–8
Mother Nature, 31
mothers, single, 88–89
Mother Teresa, 66–67, 126, 133, 157
multi-tasking, 35
Murphy, Susan, 97

nature, 6
needs, and asking, 23–24, 38–41, 118–19
niceness, 50–52
no
    allowing others to say, 39
    when to say, 90, 124, 153
nourishment, 83–84
nurturing, 22, 31

offering, 72, 78, 122, 132
Old Dogs, New Tricks, 128
opposition, 53
optimism, 139
other people, self-sufficiency in, 87–89
outside-in reform, 18–19
overwhelm, 77

paradigms, 5
partnerships, 119–29
passion, following, 21–22, 34, 65–76, 86
path of least resistance, 71
Path of Least Resistance, The, 136
patience, 30, 35, 117
patriarchal systems, 18, 36
peace, 44–45
peace at any price, Trap 5, 50–54
pearl, 100–101
Peralta, Sheila, 119, 150–51
perseverance, 33
personal life and work life, 8
perspective, 29
pleasing others, 50–52
politics, office, 57, 116–17
potential, 147
power
    accountability and, 25
    diagram, 101
    innate, 20
    loss of, 36, 40–47
    reclaiming, 95–111
    retaining, 113–19
    self-righteousness and, 39–40
    setting priorities and, 90
    sourcing, 119–29
Power Dead Even Rule, 97–98
priorities
    being your own number one priority,
        22–23, 77–93
    clarification of, 89–93
    Sourcing and, 122
problem-solving, 30, 139
productivity, 128
public speaking, 123
purpose, 56, 146

quiet, 67, 79, 116, 149

reactive mode, 135
reconnection, 8, 34
reflection of yourself in your team, 120–22
relationships
    balance and, 96–99
    belonging and, 21
    change and, 18–19
    collaboration and, 132
    feedback in, 128
    forgiveness and, 107–8
    good company in, 145–55
    power and, 95–96, 103, 114–15
    trust in, 153
rescue fantasy, 22
    Trap 4, 47–50
resentment, 40, 78, 104, 107
resilience, 35
resistance, 45–46

respect, 28–29, 125, 153
responsibility, 24–25, 106, 110, 129
results, 64
right, being, 125–26
risk-taking, 33
Roosevelt, Eleanor, 54

sabbatical, 155
safety, 58–59, 63
sarcasm, 60–61, 87
seduction, in business, 48–49
self-awareness, 3–4, 85–87
self-care, 79, 87, 92–93, 153
self-doubt, 3, 23–24
self-examination, 155
selfishness, 77
self-love, 34
self-protection, 102
    Trap 7, 58–64
self-protective strategies (SPS), 58–64
self-righteousness, 38–39, 62
self-sufficiency, in others, 87–89
servant leadership, 127
service, 122, 126–27, 144
Seven Deadly Traps, 27
    being one of the boys, 28–35
    having no voice and no choice, 40–47
    hurry, hurry, hurry, 55–58
    martyrdom, 35–40
    peace at any price, 50–54
    self-protection, 58–64
    waiting for rescue, 47–50
Sher, Barbara, 68
showing up, 34–35
single mothers, 88–89
Sir Gawain, 11–17
Sir Gromer Somer Joure, 11–14
sleep, 84–85
Sourcing, 100–101, 119–29, 158
speaking out, 36–37, 44–46, 54, 104, 118–19
speed, Trap 6, 55–58
strategies for reclaiming power
    admit mistakes and make amends, 110–11
    be accountable, 111–12
    forgive all debts, 107–10
strategies for retaining power
    be real, 116–17
    build and retain trust, 117–18
    create empowering agreements, 114–16
    remain accountable, 113–14
    speak up and speak out, 118–19
strategies for Sourcing
    be a Yes, 123–24
    give up the right to be right, 125–26
    leave everyone empowered and
        appreciated, 128–29
    surrender your ego to serve another,
        126–27

success, 68
suffering, 35–37
Sugar and Spice Rules, 50–52
surrender, service and, 126–27
survival, 35

talents, 71
teachers, 150–51
teenagers, 125–26
tension, creative, 135–43
themes in life, 75
Thiry, Kent, 118
thoughts, mastery of, 79
thumbprint of leader, 120–22
transformation, 9, 31, 92–93, 120–21, 132,
    157–58
Traps, Seven Deadly. see Seven Deadly Traps
trust
    lack of, 31, 51
    office politics and, 117–18
    in others' choices, 39–40
    partnership and, 125
    in relationships, 153
    retaining power and, 117–18
    self, 34
    sourcing and, 120–21
Turner, Tina, 105

values, 48–49
victims, 20, 24–25, 104–5, 112–13
    Trap 3, 40–47
vision, 132–44, 155

Weil, Andrew, 82
wholeness, 17
Whyte, David, 22
wildness, 21
Winfrey, Oprah, 152
win-win solutions, 54, 116, 122
wisdom, 20, 67–68, 80, 117
wise women, 68, 79, 152–53
women's movement, 5, 18, 96
Women Who Run with the Wolves, 49
work and personal life, 8
worry, 118, 137

Year to Live, A, 49
yes
    as answer to How, 143
    being a, 123–24
    when to say, 90
yoga, 82

Women Leading Women Leading Women Leading
Women Leading Women Leading Women Leading
Women Leading Women Leading Women Leading

**Want to learn more about
what it takes to be a Sovereign Leader?**

Individual Leadership Development

Women Leading Women offers two-day to one-year leadership development programs for women leaders internationally. Women Leading Women is designed to help women gain their freedom and choice—in short, to become more clear and powerful, able to effect the kinds of changes that serve us all.

Organization Initiatives for Women

Through our comprehensive women's leadership initiatives, we support organizations committed to the advancement of women. Let our team of skilled organizational consultants provide you with all the tools needed to create a successful program for women leaders.

For more information about this and other program offerings, please see our website

www.dedehenley.com

The Secret of Sovereignty
Women Choosing Leadership at Work and in Life

Order by phone: 1.888.655.8728
Order by mail: Secret of Sovereignty/Ragnelle Press
                 17837 First Ave. S. #302
                 Seattle, WA 98148
Order online: www.DedeHenley.com

QUANTITY	TITLE	PRICE	CAN. PRICE	TOTAL
	The Secret of Sovereignty by Dede Henley	$19.95 Hardcover	$23.95 Hardcover	

Shipping & Handling, add $5.95

Sales Tax (WA state residents only, add 8.9%)

TOTAL ENCLOSED

Method of Payment

☐ Visa   ☐ MasterCard   ☐ Check or money order

_____   _____ / _____
Card Number   Exp. Date

_____
Signature

_____
Name

_____
Address

_____
City   State   Zip

_____
Phone   Fax

Quantity discounts available.
For more information on books and workshops for leaders,
inquire at www.DedeHenley.com.
Thank you for your order!